ELEGANT SMALL HOMES
OF THE TWENTIES

99 Designs from a Competition

Chicago Tribune

With a new introduction by
Daniel D. Reiff

DOVER PUBLICATIONS, INC.
Mineola, New York

Bibliographical Note

This Dover edition, first published in 2008, was originally published as the *Chicago Tribune Book of Homes,* Chicago Tribune, in 1927. A new introduction by Daniel D. Reiff has been prepared for this edition.

Library of Congress Cataloging-in-Publication Data

Elegant small homes of the twenties : 99 designs from a competition / Chicago Tribune.
    p. cm.
  Originally published: Chicago tribune book of homes. c1927.
  ISBN-13: 978-0-486-46910-2 (pbk.)
  ISBN-10: 0-486-46910-7
    1. Architecture, Domestic—United States—Designs and plans. 2. Architecture, Domestic—United States—20th century—Designs and plans. I. Chicago Tribune (Firm) II. Title.
NA7208.C45 2008
728.0973'09042—dc22

2008028455

Manufactured in the United States of America
Dover Publications, Inc., 31 East 2nd Street, Mineola, N.Y. 11501

Introduction to the Dover Edition

by Daniel D. Reiff, PhD

If a middle- or upper-middle-class family in the Chicago area wanted to have a five- or six-room house erected for themselves in 1927, what were their options? Although one's first inclination might be to "consult an architect or builder," there were in fact a number of choices—some quite economical—open to them.

One route would have been, after consulting a house-plan book, to order the plans and specifications for their home from a mail-order plan company. These had existed for well over a century: The first mail-order plans seem to date to 1856, and the service grew energetically through the late-nineteenth and early-twentieth centuries. In the Chicago area two of the most popular firms providing a great variety of plans were The Radford Architectural Co., and the Home Builders Catalog Co. [1]

Another possibility was to order plans from companies that also supplied low-cost building materials (except for masonry portions of the house), cut and fitted to the exact specifications of the house selected. This pre-cut system had been begun by The Aladdin Co. of Bay City, Michigan, about 1908; Sears, Roebuck and Co. also began selling such pre-cut houses in 1918 (prior to then they supplied "enough lumber to build the house," but it was not pre-cut). By the 1920s there were quite a number of such firms who would supply the blueprints and all necessary construction documents along with the material, cut and fitted by machinery at the factory—which would save the local carpenter (still using hand tools in the 1920s) a great deal of labor. [2]

One could also simply consult a local carpenter, builder, or contractor, who would have catalogs of house designs one could choose from—or just take a design from a magazine, or a photo of a house one liked, to him—and he could work up drawings, with appropriate customizing, from that.

But naturally, one of the best methods, to assure getting the most sophisticated design adapted to one's specific needs, was to consult a professional architect. This was usually the most expensive, however, as the "standard" rate for plans, specifications, and superintendence of the construction, was at least five percent of the building's cost. [3] That is where books of "architect designed" house plans came into the picture—either from firms like Radford (whose architects were all "licensed in the State of Illinois"), or from specialized publications of architects' house designs...such as that published in 1927 by the *Chicago Tribune.*

Like many newspapers of the day, the *Chicago Tribune* had a Home Builders' Department, the aim of which was to provide information to its readers on home building, interior decoration, and to publish the occasional house plan for inspiration to those about to build. This volume of ninety-nine skillfully drawn designs, however, was something special: all were five- and six-room houses that could be built for about $7,500—a fairly substantial sum in those days, but affordable to middle- and upper-middle-class families.[4] Their main purpose was to give readers a comprehensive idea of what could be built, in a "fireproof" house, for that sum. [5]

The *Tribune* held a national competition to amass all these charming designs. In 1926 they must have put notices of the competition in national newspapers, and in trade publications, for they received entries from all over the country: There are designs from Portland, Maine, New Haven, Conn., Sarasota, Florida; from Buffalo, Indianapolis, and Kansas City; and from Tacoma, San Francisco, and Los Angeles. Major cities had the most entries: New York City with 20, Chicago with 14, and Detroit with 8; 29 municipalities had just one submission. With the ninety-nine designs coming from 18 states, it was certainly a nationwide competition. [6]

As a way of amassing designs meeting a particular program, competitions had been popular in America for almost half a century. *The American Architect and Building News* (Boston) held one in 1882 for a seven-room house (to cost about $3,000), with a great many of the designs subsequently published in their journal. They held another competition in 1883 for a small house to cost $1,500; the next year one for a double house, to cost $3,000; and in 1885 for a $5,000 house. *Carpentry and Building,* another professional journal, held competitions for house designs in 1884 and 1893, and in 1898 one for houses in three different price ranges. *Architectural Forum* (New York) was also a sponsor of architectural design competitions.

But it was the building materials organizations—to encourage home owners and builders to use their particular product—that sponsored the most competitions for house designs. The Association of American Portland Cement (Philadelphia) held one in 1907. In a 1910 house plan catalog the Building Brick Association of America states that the plans were "a selection from more than 800 drawings submitted in a competition," and their plan catalog of 1912 drew its designs from 666 entries in a competition. Almost every building-trade organization of the day held competitions for house designs of various sizes, as mentioned in their house plan catalogs, for example: National Fire Proofing Co., Philadelphia, 1912; Hydraulic-Press Brick Co., St. Louis, 1914; American Face Brick Association, Chicago, 1920; United States Gypsum Co., Chicago, 1925; California Redwood Association, San Francisco, 1925; Weyerhaeuser Forest Products, St. Paul, 1926. From their catalogs one could purchase low-price plans and specifications of the houses illustrated—utilizing their particular product, of course.

The *Chicago Tribune* compendium of designs was different, however. Monetary prizes were awarded for the nine best five-room houses, and for the ten best six-room houses. The *Tribune* provided "complete working plans, including blueprints and specifications," however, for only *three* of them: the first prize for the five-room house, and the first and second prize six-room houses. The plans cost only $1 each (or "$1.15 by mail")—a real bargain, since the usual mail-order house plans from organizations such as Standard Homes Company cost $20, and of course custom-designed house plans by an architect—though it would include superintending construction too—would probably be five percent of the cost, or $375 for any of the *Tribune* designs.

If a reader, or a contractor, wanted to build one of those three prize-winning designs, he was in luck; but what of the other ninety-six designs, some of which might be more appealing than the prize-winning ones? [7] Here the reader had two viable options. One

was to write to the architect who prepared the published design to order the plans, or prepare something similar adapted to the exact specifications of the prospective home owner. This was surely what most of the architects submitting designs hoped would happen, and their addresses are prominently listed with each design.

But the prospective home owner might also simply take one of these designs to a local builder or contractor, who could easily work up specifications from the details and dimensions given on each plate, and thus build a "bootleg" copy of the original design. This was, after all, how house designs in books had been used in America since 1738, when Drayton Hall was erected following a plate in Palladio's *Quattro Libri;* how Samuel McIntire used plates in pattern books by Asher Benjamin and William Pain to create his Gardner House in 1804; and how countless builders and carpenters copied—freely or meticulously—A. J. Downing's famous gothic cottage design of 1842 all across America.

The designs provided by the *Tribune* volume were varied. Many were based on the English vernacular, and some reflected the reformist mode of Charles Voysey; some had half-timbering details, or a touch of English Regency style. Many had references to American colonial, or Spanish southwest forms, and a few were "modern" in their cubic severity. But none was too far from popular tastes. Whether one used these designs for general inspiration, purchased working drawings from the original architect, or had a local contractor erect a copy—or variant—of the design, one could be assured of a professional plan and design that would stand the test of time. [8]

Were any of these houses actually built? Now that this volume is being reprinted, it will be interesting to see if some of these charming houses can be found in the Chicago area—or further afield. But it does seem that these appealing models had an impact on other designers. For example, the hipped-roof house on p. 93 certainly could be the inspiration for the similar dwelling in Robert Jones's *Small Homes of Architectural Distinction* (1929), p. 270. (This volume was reprinted by Dover in 1987 as *Authentic Small Houses of the Twenties,* Dover 0-486-25406-2.) Several other designs appear to be models for homes published by the Plan Service Company, St. Paul, in their *Ideal Homes (11th ed.)*: *Two-Story Houses of the 1930s.* Such well-designed, and historically allusive homes do have a perennial appeal.

1. The first mail-order plans for houses seem to be those advertised by Cleaveland, Backus and Backus in their 1856 book of house designs, *Village and Farm Cottages.* Soon others followed: Cummings and Miller in 1865, and, in the 1870s George Palliser and also E. C. Hussey. In the 1880s books of house designs by R. W. Shoppell, and George F. Barber, all offered plans for sale; by 1898 one of the most prolific companies, the Chicago firm which became The Radford Architectural Company, was offering mail-order plans too. In the early twentieth century there were a vast number of such firms, Standard Homes Company of Washington, DC (beginning about 1921), and Home Builders Catalog Co., Chicago (beginning in 1926), among the most popular and prolific. The plans provided could be for frame, for face brick (on frame construction), solid brick, or concrete dwellings. (The *Home Builders Catalog* had a national popularity; the 1927 copy I consulted is inscribed with the name of an owner in Lexington, Kentucky.)

2. Though Chicago, because of its excellent lake and rail connections, was a center for this sort of business, other national firms were also prominent in the 1920s, such as the Ray H. Bennett Lumber Co. in Tonawanda, New York, and the Gordon-Van Tine Co. of Davenport, Iowa. Of course this system was for *frame* houses, and the stonework or concrete (for foundations), or brick for chimneys, was explicitly excluded.

3. The traditional architect's fee of five percent based on the total cost of construction, included "plans and specifications, detail drawings, and superintendence," was set out in print by Calvert Vaux in his 1857 book *Villas and Cottages,* but the five percent schedule seems to go back to at least 1800. The rate was confirmed by the American Institute of Architects in 1866. Some mail-order architectural designers, such as George Palliser, charged only two percent for designs and specifications, but this did not, of course, include superintendence of construction. Today, an architect might charge six percent for plans and drawings only (some specifications included on them)—but twice that if details for mechanicals and supervision, were to be included. In the 1920s, however, there seem to have been quite a lot of flexibility. In a 1928 catalog (*Honor Bilt Modern Homes,* p. 17), Sears claimed that for "dwellings costing less than $10,000.00" architectural firms would charge "10 percent...on the completed cost."

4. A first glance this seems like a preposterously low amount for a house, but because of inflation, and the great rise in Americans' standard of living, the dollar in those days was obviously "worth more" than today. For example (drawing from a 1926 *National Geographic*—the year that the competition was advertised) we find that a four-door Dodge sedan cost from $895 to $995; a Chrysler cost from $1,395 to $1,895; and a Cadillac cost $2,995. Though of course automotive amenities are different today, multiplying by 12 give a rough idea of current costs; thus the $7,500 house would be about $90,000 today.

5. The competition guidelines specified the exact lot size (30 by 125 feet), the total cubic content (23,000 cu. ft. or less), and apparently that exterior walls were to be built of fireproof materials. These, as listed in each design's specifications, include brick, stone (often identified as "limestone," "local stone," "square rubble laid at random courses," etc.), stucco on tile (or brick), poured concrete, "hollow terra cotta," concrete, with one specified as "8 inch cinder block, stuccoed." (Window sashes were often noted to be steel; and one architect even specified that interior framing was to be of "metal lumber.") Roofs too (except for three: two of wood shingles and one... thatched!) were fireproof, given as slate, "heavy asbestos shingles," or tile. And it's just as well the houses were largely fireproof: The space between the dwelling and the lot line was usually only about three feet, so an adjacent house might be only six feet away!

6. Entries came from forty different municipalities, in the following states: California, Connecticut, Florida, Illinois, Indiana, Maine, Massachusetts, Michigan, Missouri, New Jersey, New York, North Carolina, North Dakota, Ohio, Oregon, Pennsylvania, Washington, and Wisconsin.

7. Somewhat mysteriously, the first prize five-room house, an English Regency inspired design, had exterior walls capped with a low parapet, *with a hidden eaves trough behind it,* running around the entire house. This treatment, while satisfactory in places where it does not freeze in winter (as in London, where this feature was invented in the early eighteenth century as a mode of fireproofing city dwellings), would be a disaster in Chicago. Without annual inspection and cleaning, hidden eaves troughs of this sort will eventually crack and allow standing water to penetrate the exterior wall, spalling the masonry, and rotting out the rafter ends just below.

8. The national popularity of the *Tribune* book is suggested by the fact that the copy I used to prepare this introduction was formerly owned by the "consulting interior decorator" Earl Hart Miller, a well-known authority in Dallas, Texas.

Daniel D. Reiff, PhD, is the author of *Houses from Books: Treatises, Pattern Books, and Catalogs in American Architecture, 1738-1950, A History and Guide* (Pennsylvania State University Press, 2000), which won the 2001 Historic Preservation Book Prize from the Center for Historic Preservation, Mary Washington College, Fredericksburg, Virginia.

Ideal Homes, p. 54, a parallel to the
Tribune design on p. 12.

Ideal Homes, p. 55, possibly inspired
by the *Tribune* design on p. 27.

Ideal Homes, p. 32, possibly inspired
by the *Tribune* design on p. 85.

Introduction to the 1927 Edition

The small house of today is improving rapidly. Where formerly the attention of skilled architects was seldom given to the house of modest dimensions, we now find trained men of talent incorporating into the small home ideas of real worth, types of rare charm and the best possible plans for comfort and convenience.

The designs published in this book, a chosen few from among the many submitted to The Chicago Tribune in its Homes Competition, reveal the present trend of domestic architecture in our country; that movement which seeks to draw inspiration for small homes as well as large ones from the accumulated art of generations past and from sources widely separate.

Few of these homes boast any strict adherence to period form, but accentuate rather the elements of interesting design. A strong effort is made towards the creation of those types which are most truly representative of our complex life.

There is one very definite advantage to be enjoyed from choosing for one's home a house plan which a recognized architect has drawn up, not for any one family alone, but rather for general public approval. The majority of the drawings this book offers possess this advantage! It too often happens that the individual ideas are too exclusively personal to give to the house a practical, general appeal. This means that in case the owner wishes to dispose of his house in a few years he will find that he as strayed too far from the average taste and the resale value of his home greatly lessened.

The designs shown in this book keep close to generally accepted principles. While they satisfy artistically they conform practically to the general mass desire.

Architecture has followed varying roads in this country for the last two centuries. Formerly our architecture was almost completely subject to English, French, Dutch, and Spanish influence. These different nationalities brought to our country their own architectural preferences. The early supremacy of the English made itself felt architecturally, so that by the time of the formation of the thirteen colonies our domestic architecture was Colonial in character.

We find it possible today to design our homes in an infinite variety of styles. We have dozens of materials to incorporate into our homes and hundreds of appliances to utilize to improve our living conditions.

In this book will be found the formal Colonial of New England, the gracious Colonial of the Southern states, the purposely unsymmetrical and picturesque homes of the English cottage types and the quaintly artistic Normandy and Brittany dwellings. There are examples too of the stately ornate French, the Italian, the softly appealing Spanish.

If, in the study of this book, some spark of that striving and that inspiration which has gone into its drawing strikes a chord responsive in others, if the homes amid its pages reach out and make their appeal, bringing men and women a step beyond there dream home and a step closer to their real one, then surely its mission will have been accomplished.

LOUISE BARGELT
HOME BUILDERS' DEPARTMENT
CHICAGO TRIBUNE

Designs

PAGE

1st Prize Winner—Five Room House—WILLIAM J. O'CONNOR 11
2nd Prize Winner—Five Room House—GEORGE D. CONNER 12
3rd Prize Winner—Five Room House—H. ROY KELLEY 13
4th Prize Winner—Five Room House—HILLARD RUSSELL 14
5th Prize Winner—Five Room House—JOHN PAUL TURNER 15
6th Prize Winner—Five Room House—ANTHONY WUCHTERL 16
7th Prize Winner—Five Room House—CLARENCE W. HUNT 17
8th Prize Winner—Five Room House—RUSSELL E. YATES-E. WAYNE YATES 18
9th Prize Winner—Five Room House—ANGUS McD. McSWEENEY 19
9th Prize Winner—Five Room House—ANGUS McD. McSWEENEY 20
1st Prize Winner—Six Room House—RICHARD E. BISHOP 21
2nd Prize Winner—Six Room House—AMEDEO LEONE 22
3rd Prize Winner—Six Room House—LOUIS C. ROSENBERG-G. DEWEY SWAN 23
4th Prize Winner—Six Room House—PIERRE-WRIGHT 24
5th Prize Winner—Six Room House—H. R. BISHOP 25
6th Prize Winner—Six Room House—CONSTANTIN ALEXANDRE PERTZOFF 26
7th Prize Winner—Six Room House—WILLIAM P. HELLEN-BURWELL F. HAMRICK 27
8th Prize Winner—Six Room House—EDWARD D. JAMES-JOSEPH D. SMALL 28
9th Prize Winner—Six Room House—W. F. MULLAY 29
10th Prize Winner—Six Room House—OWEN LAU. GOWMAN 30
Five Room House—HELMER N. ANDERSON 31
Five Room House—ARTHUR F. DEAM 32
Five Room House—JAMES D. WICKENDEN 33
Five Room House—MARIO CIAMPI 34
Five Room House—MAYOL H. LINSCOTT 35
Five Room House—W. RAY WINEGAR 36
Five Room House—W. G. BYRNE 37
Five Room House—R. VANBUREN LIVINGSTON 38
Five Room House—CLARENCE B. MACKAY-GEORGE F. AXT 39
Five Room House—EDGAR ALBRIGHT 40
Five Room House—H. A. SURMAN 41
Five Room House—ROBERT V. WADE-FRED J. ABENDROTH 42
Five Room House—CHARLES MULLER 43
Five Room House—ROBERT KILMARTIN 44
Five Room House—JOHN FIORITO 45
Five Room House—HARRY L. WAGNER 46
Five Room House—W. PELL PULIS 47
Five Room House—WILLIAM B. MILLWARD 48
Five Room House—JOHN RHINELANDER 49
Five Room House—CLYDE E. LIGHT 50
Five Room House—JAMES W. MINICK-M. DALE SMITH 51
Five Room House—PAUL F. MANN 52
Five Room House—GEORGE L. RAMSEY 53
Five Room House—HERBERT A. MAGOON 54
Five Room House—H. G. LEWIS 55
Five Room House—SHIRLEY CLEMENTS HORSLEY 56
Five Room House—ELMER WILLIAM MARX 57
Five Room House—JAMES R. MILLS 58

PAGE

Five Room House—WILLIAM A. ROLLESTON 59
Five Room House—LEWIS A. SIBERZ 60
Five Room House—ONNIE MANNKI 61
Five Room House—CHARLES A. MARKLEY 62
Five Room House—WILLARD C. WALKER 63
Five Room House—RIPLEY-LEBOUTILLIER 64
Five Room House—J. PENDLEBURY 65
Five Room House—W. PHELPS CUNNINGHAM 66
Five Room House—ERNEST IRVING FREESE 67
Five Room House—CARL JENSEN 68
Five Room House—GEORGE L. EKVALL 69
Five Room House—JOHN J. BRESEE 70
Five Room House—S. M. SPROULE 71
Five Room House—J. H. RAFTERY 72
Five Room House—RICHARD L. CARTWRIGHT 73
Five Room House—PIERRE-WRIGHT 74
Five Room House—J. FLOYD YEWELL 75
Five Room House—EARNEST R. ARMSTRONG 76
Five Room House—ARTHUR J. POHLE 77
Five Room House—I. C. BAROUSSE 78
Five Room House—THOMAS F. ROWE 79
Five Room House—NORMAN T. MAXOM 80
Five Room House—WALTER T. ROLFE 81
Five Room House—WM. R. WEIGLER 82
Six Room House—W. E. ANDERSON-E. C. JORGENSEN 83
Six Room House—WILLIAM E. ASH 84
Six Room House—J. LEONARD RUSH 85
Six Room House—THOMAS W. COOPER 86
Six Room House—RIPLEY-LEBOUTILIER 87
Six Room House—THEODORE H. WESSEL 88
Six Room House—ALEXANDER BERESNIAKOFF 89
Six Room House—RAYMOND MILES STOWELL 90
Six Room House—DANIEL E. SHEA 91
Six Room House—HAROLD A. RICH 92
Six Room House—JOHN ENGLAND, JR. 93
Six Room House—GEORGE F. AXT-CLARENCE B. MACKAY 94
Six Room House—FRANCIS KEALLY 95
Six Room House—JOHN DONALD TUTTLE 96
Six Room House—LEO. J. MALATESTA-WILLIAM STEWART 97
Six Room House—ALFRED COOKMAN CASS 98
Six Room House—WAKEFIELD WORCESTER 99
Six Room House—LESLIE F. AYRES 100
Six Room House—ANTONIO DI NARDO and ALVIN HANKE 101
Six Room House—PHILIP O. SAXE 102
Six Room House—JOHN RICHARD ROWE 103
Six Room House—EDGAR CIBERSON and L. F. ANDERSON 104
Six Room House—RAYMOND A. FISHER 105
Six Room House—DEXTER EDGARTON 106
Six Room House—RALPH W. HAMMETT 107
Six Room House—THAYNE J. LOGAN 108
Six Room House—HOWARD EMSLEY IRWIN 109
Six Room House—KEITH S. HEINE 110

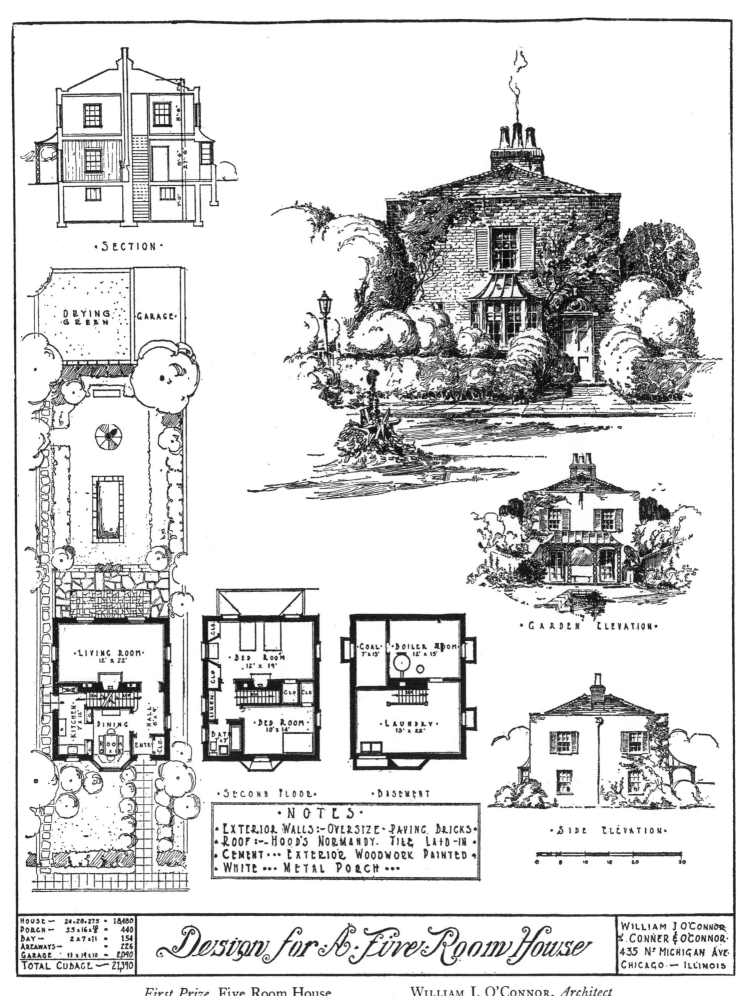

· SECTION ·

DRYING GREEN   GARAGE

· LIVING ROOM ·
12' x 22'

KITCHEN
7' x 12'

DINING ROOM
10' x 12'   HALL
6' x 9'   ENTRY CLO.

· SECOND FLOOR ·

CLO. CLO.

BED ROOM
12' x 19'

LINEN CLO.

CLO. CLO.

BED ROOM
10' x 14'

BATH

· BASEMENT ·

COAL
7' x 15'   BOILER ROOM
12' x 15'

LAUNDRY
13' x 22'

· GARDEN ELEVATION ·

· SIDE ELEVATION ·

0   5   10   15   20   30

· N O T E S ·
· EXTERIOR WALLS:—OVERSIZE PAVING BRICKS·
· ROOF:—HOOD'S NORMANDY TILE LAID-IN·
· CEMENT ··· EXTERIOR WOODWORK PAINTED·
· WHITE ··· METAL PORCH ···

HOUSE—	24·28·275 =	18480
PORCH—	55 x 16 x ½ =	440
BAY—	2 x 7 x 11 =	154
AREAWAYS—		226
GARAGE	11 x 14 x 10 =	2,090
TOTAL CUBAGE —		21,390

Design for A Five Room House

WILLIAM J O'CONNOR
℅ CONNER & O'CONNOR·
435 N° MICHIGAN AVE·
CHICAGO — ILLINOIS

First Prize, Five Room House   .   .   .   WILLIAM J. O'CONNOR, *Architect*

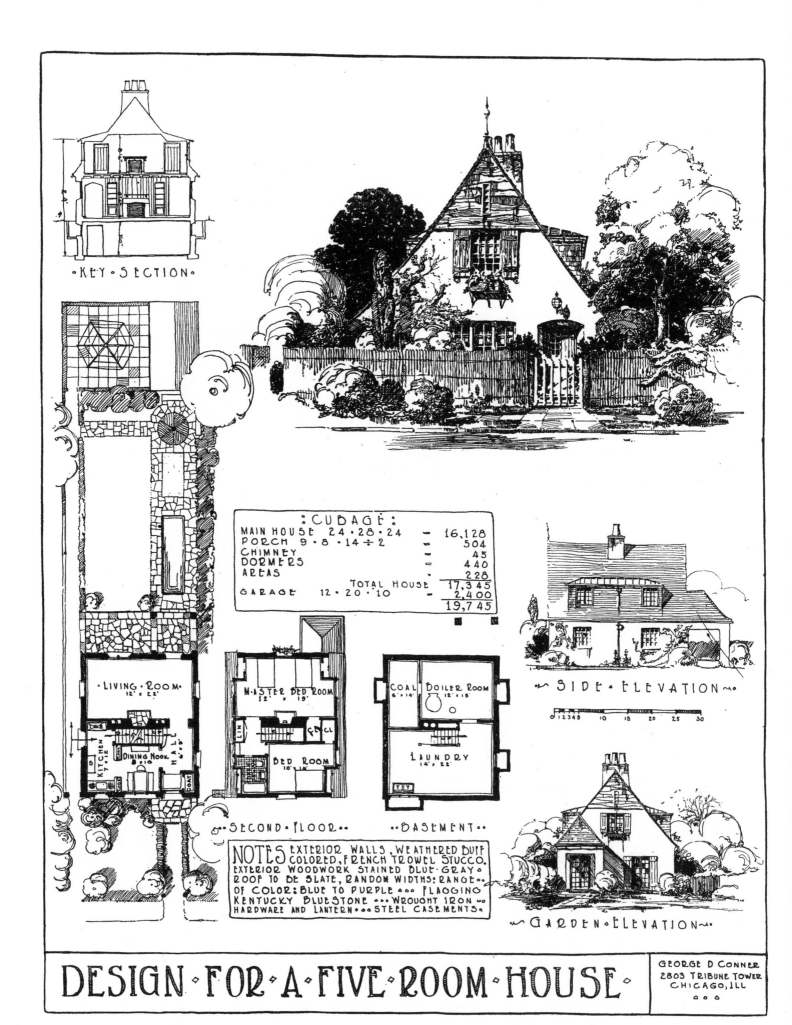

·KEY·SECTION·

:CUBAGE:

MAIN HOUSE 24·28·24	=	16,128
PORCH 9·8·14÷2	=	504
CHIMNEY	=	45
DORMERS	=	440
AREAS		228
	TOTAL HOUSE	17,345
GARAGE 12·20·10	=	2,400
		19,745

·SIDE·ELEVATION·

0 1 2 3 4 5   10   15   20   25   30

·LIVING·ROOM·
12' x 22'

KITCHEN
DINING·NOOK 8'10
HALL

M·ASTER·BED·ROOM·
12' x 19'

LIN CL

BED ROOM
10' x 14'

·SECOND·FLOOR·

COAL
6' x 14'
BOILER·ROOM
12' x 18'

LAUNDRY
14' x 22'

·BASEMENT·

NOTES EXTERIOR WALLS, WEATHERED BUFF COLORED, FRENCH TROWEL STUCCO. EXTERIOR WOODWORK STAINED BLUE·GRAY ROOF TO BE SLATE, RANDOM WIDTHS; RANGE OF COLOR: BLUE TO PURPLE ••• FLAGGING KENTUCKY BLUESTONE ••• WROUGHT IRON HARDWARE AND LANTERN •• STEEL CASEMENTS.

·GARDEN·ELEVATION·

DESIGN·FOR·A·FIVE·ROOM·HOUSE·

GEORGE D CONNER
2803 TRIBUNE TOWER
CHICAGO, ILL
◦◦◦

Second Prize, Five Room House . . . GEORGE D. CONNER, *Architect*

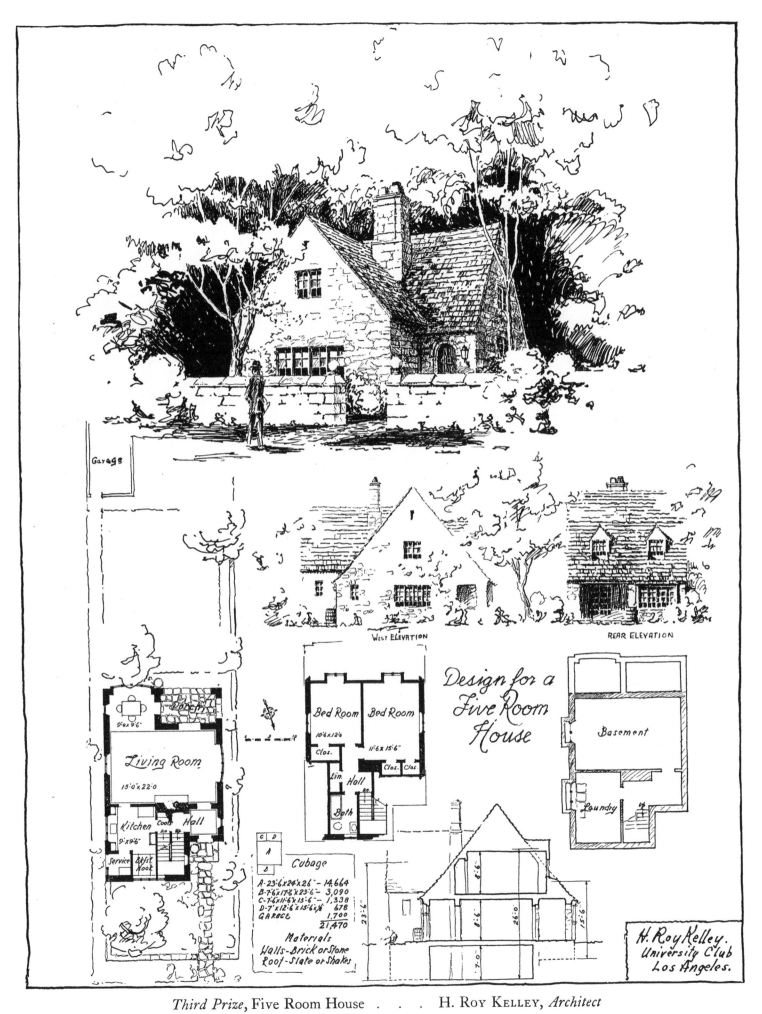

Garage

WEST ELEVATION

REAR ELEVATION

Porch

9'0"x9'6"

Living Room

15'0"x22'0"

Kitchen

9'x9'6"

Cook

Hall

Service

Bkfst Nook

Bed Room

10'6"x12'0"

Clos.

Bed Room

11'6"x15'6"

Clos. Clos.

Lin. Hall

Bath

Design for a Five Room House

Basement

Laundry

C D
A
B

Cubage

A-23'6"x24"x26" - 14,664
B-7'6"x17'6"x23'6" - 3,090
C-7'6"x11'6"x15'6" - 1,338
D-7'x12'6"x15'6"x½ - 678
GARAGE - 1,700
21,470

Materials
Walls-Brick or Stone
Roof-Slate or Shakes

23'6"

6'6"

6'6" 26'0" 15'6"

7'0"

H. Roy Kelley.
University Club
Los Angeles.

Third Prize, Five Room House . . . H. Roy Kelley, *Architect*

DESIGN FOR A FIVE ROOM HOUSE

CUBAGE
21.5 x 49 x 17 = 17,910
21.5 x 7 x 18 = 2,709
6.5 x 8 x 23 = 598
TOTAL 21,217

NOTES.
EXTERIOR -
WALLS OF
STONE ROOF
OF SLATE OR
DARK WOOD SH-
INGLES EXT-
ERIOR WOODWO-
RK NATURAL-
PINE

SECTION.

GARAGE
9'6" x 18'0"

LAUNDRY
11'6" x 14'6"

VEGETABLE
STORAGE
6'0" x 8'0"

BOILER ROOM
STORAGE
15'0" x 23'0"

VEGETABLE GARDEN

CHAMBER
9'0" x 11'0"

CHAMBER
10'6" x 13'0"

CLO. CLO.

BATH

CLO. CLO.

KITCHEN
7'6" x 10'6"

LIVING ROOM
15'0" x 21'0"

HILLARD RUSSELL
625 LEXINGTON AVE
NEW YORK CITY

SOUTH-WEST

NORTH-WEST

NORTH-EAST

SOUTH-EAST

Fourth Prize, Five Room House   .   .   .   .   HILLARD RUSSELL, *Architect*

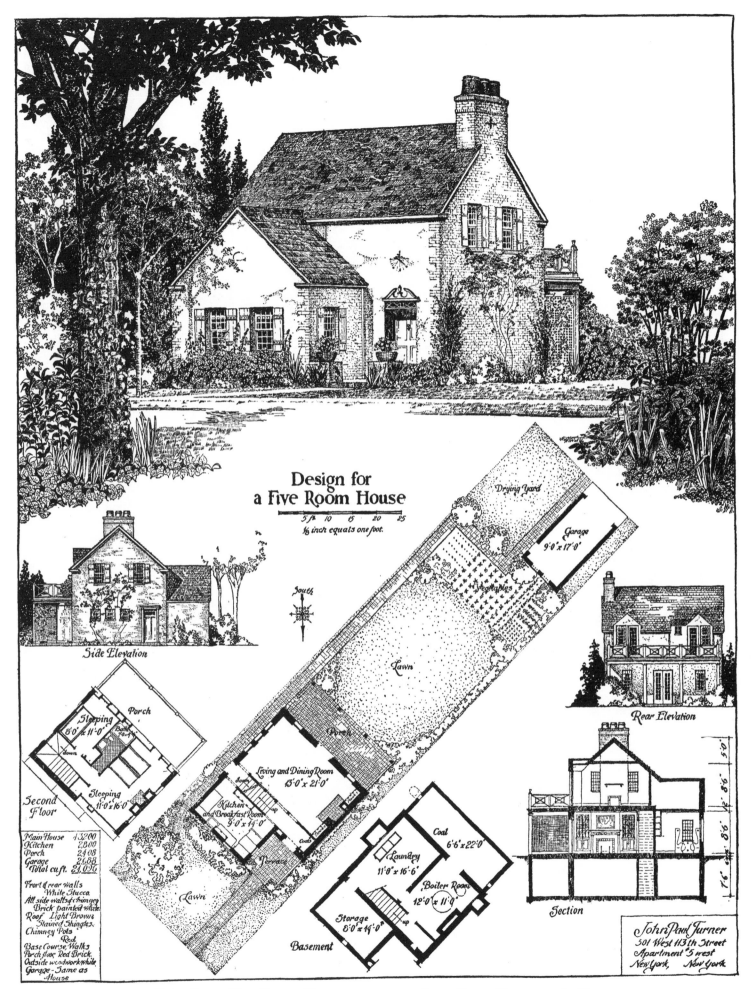

Design for
a Five Room House

5 ft 10 15 20 25

⅛ inch equals one foot.

South

Drying Yard

Garage
9'0" x 17'0"

Vegetables

Lawn

Side Elevation

Rear Elevation

Second Floor

Sleeping
8'0" x 11'0"

Porch

Bath

down

Sleeping
11'0" x 16'0"

Porch

Living and Dining Room
15'0" x 21'0"

Kitchen
and Breakfast Room
9'0" x 14'0"

Terrace

Lawn

Coal
6'6" x 22'0"

Laundry
11'0" x 16'6"

Boiler Room
12'0" x 11'0"

Storage
8'0" x 14'0"

Basement

Section

Main House	13200
Kitchen	2800
Porch	2408
Garage	2608
Total cu.ft.	21,096

Front & rear walls
White Stucco.
All side walls & chimney
Brick painted white.
Roof Light Brown
Stained Shingles.
Chimney Pots
Red.
Base Course, Walks
Porch floor, Red Brick.
Outside woodwork white
Garage - Same as
House

John Paul Turner
501 West 113th Street
Apartment 5 west
New York, New York

Fifth Prize, Five Room House . . . JOHN PAUL TURNER, *Architect*

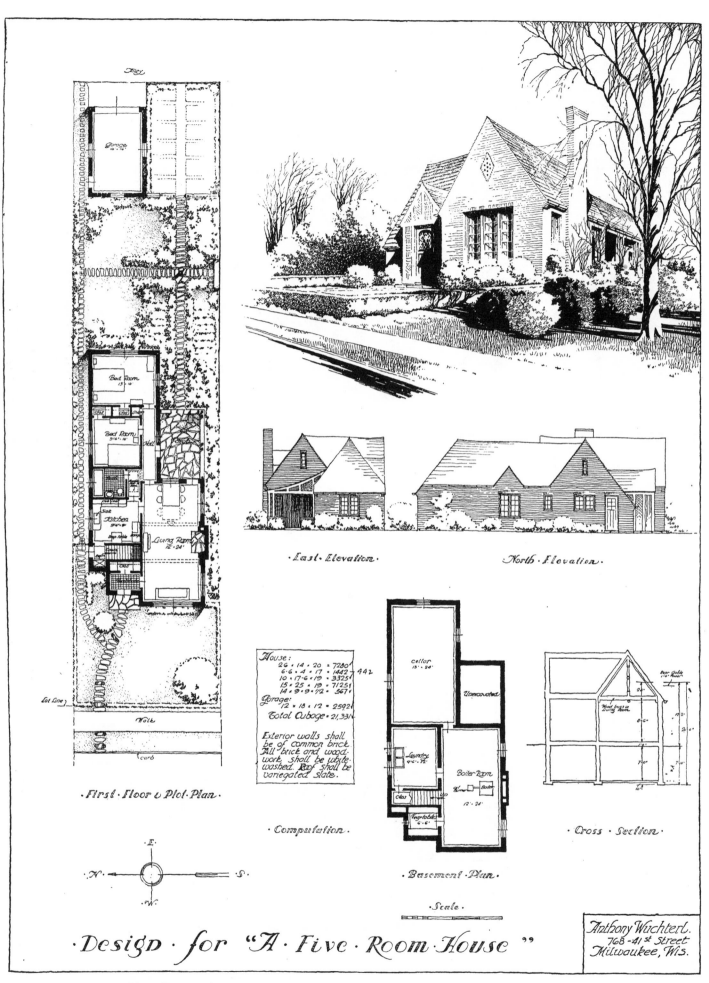

Alley

Garage
10 × 18

Bed Room
13 × 10

Bed Room
11'-6" × 10'

Kitchen
9'-6" × 8'

Living Room
12 × 24

Lot Line

Walk

Curb

·First·Floor ↄ Plot·Plan·

·*East·Elevation*·   ·*North·Elevation*·

House:
26 · 14 · 20 = 7280
66 · 4 · 17 = 1442 ⎱ 442
10 · 17-6 · 19 = 3325 ⎰
15 · 25 · 19 = 7125
14 · 9 · 9 · 1/2 = 567

Garage:
12 · 18 · 12 = 2592
Total Cubage = 21,331

Exterior walls shall
be of common brick.
All brick and wood-
work shall be white-
washed. Roof shall be
variegated slate.

·*Computation*·

Cellar
13 · 24

Uncovered

Laundry
9'-6" · 12'

Boiler Room
12 · 24

Gas

Vegetables
6 · 6'

·*Basement·Plan*·

·*Cross·Section*·

Scale

E
N · — · S
W

Anthony Wuchterl
768 - 41st Street
Milwaukee, Wis.

·Design · for "A · Five · Room · House"

Sixth Prize, Five Room House . . . ANTHONY WUCHTERL, *Architect*

DESIGN FOR A FIVE ROOM HOUSE

Seventh Prize, Five Room House . . . CLARENCE W. HUNT, *Architect*

[17]

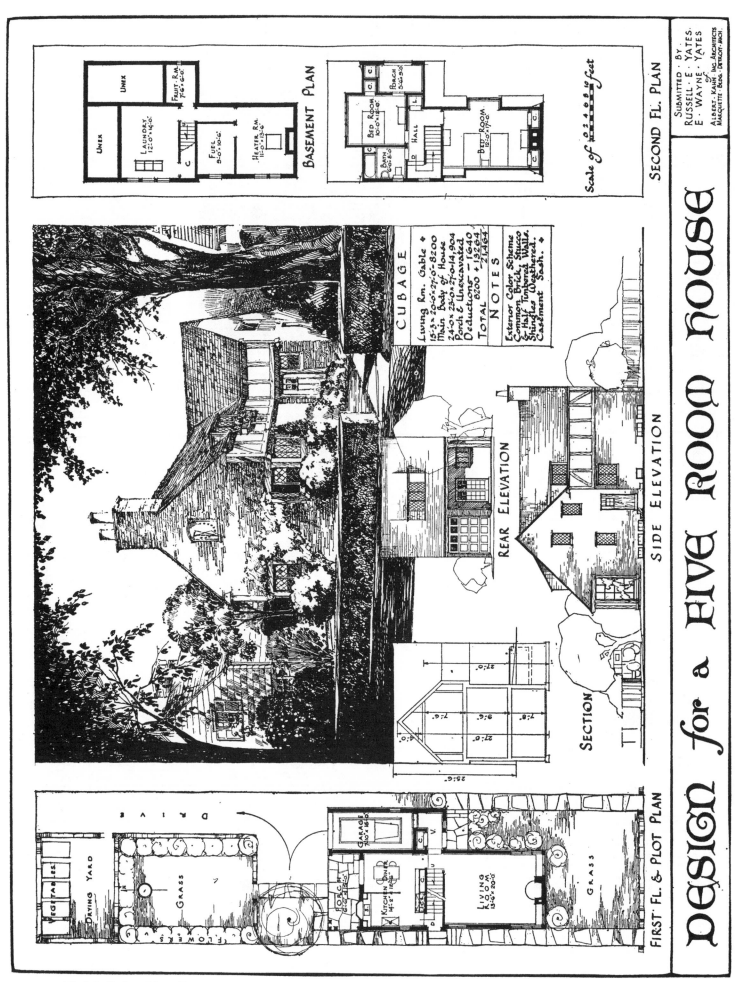

Design for a Five Room House

Eighth Prize, Five Room House . . . Russell E. Yates and E. Wayne Yates, *Architects*

· DESIGN FOR A FIVE ROOM HOVSE ·

ANGVS Mᶜ D. Mᶜ SWEENEY.
250 SANTA PAVLA AVE.
SAN FRANCISCO
CALIFORNIA.

Ninth Prize, Five Room House . . . Angus McD. McSweeney, *Architect*

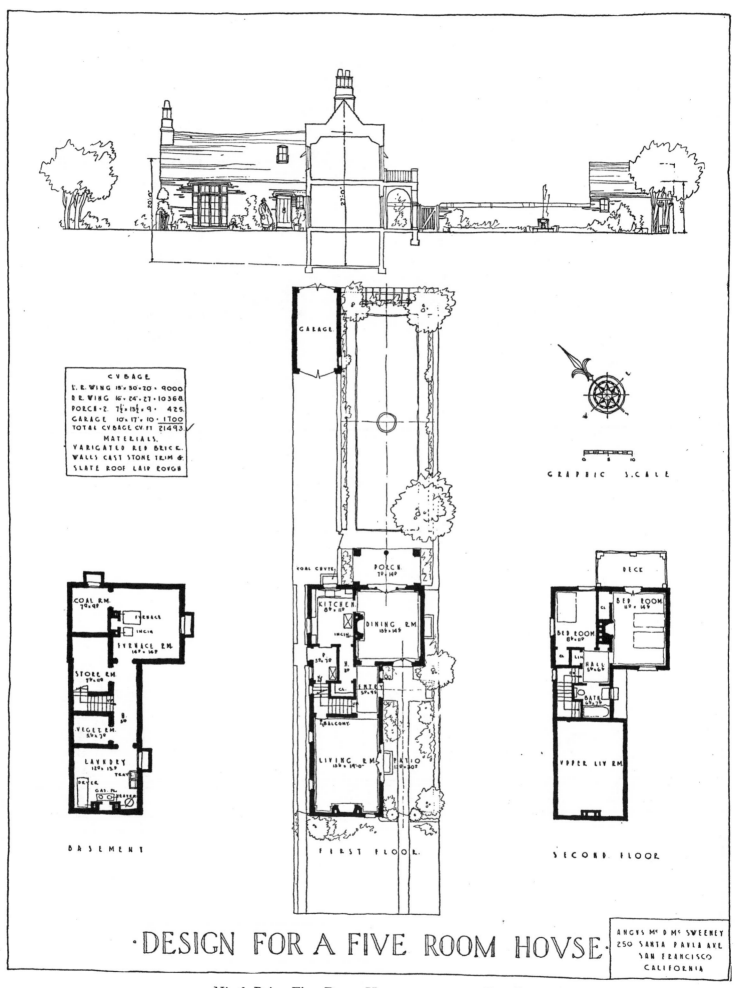

CVBAGE
L. R. WING 15'×30'×20' · 9000.
D. R. WING 16'×24'×27' · 10368.
PORCH · 2. 7½×13½×9 · 425.
GARAGE 10'×17'×10 · 1700
TOTAL CVBAGE CV. FT 21493.
MATERIALS.
VARIGATED RED BRICK.
WALLS CAST STONE TRIM &
SLATE ROOF LAID ROVGH

GRAPHIC SCALE

GARAGE.

COAL CHVTE.   PORCH 7'9"×14'9"

COAL RM. 7'9"×9'9"   FURNACE   INCIN

FURNACE RM. 14'9"×16'9"

STORE RM. 7'9"×11'9"

VEGET. RM. 5'9"×7'9"

LAVNDRY 12'9"×13'9"   TRAYS

DRYER   GAS PL.   HEATER

BASEMENT

KITCHEN 8'9"×11'9"
INCIN
DINING RM. 13'9"×14'9"

ENTRY 5'9"×9'9"
BALCONY.

LIVING RM. 13'9"×19'-0"   PATIO 12'9"×30'9"

FIRST FLOOR.

DECK

BED ROOM 11'9"×14'9"

BED ROOM 8'9"×11'9"

HALL 5'9"×6'9"

BATH 6'9"×7'9"

UPPER LIV RM.

SECOND FLOOR

·DESIGN FOR A FIVE ROOM HOVSE·

ANGVS MᶜD MᶜSWEENEY
250 SANTA PAVLA AVE
SAN FRANCISCO
CALIFORNIA

Ninth Prize, Five Room House . . . Detail

[20]

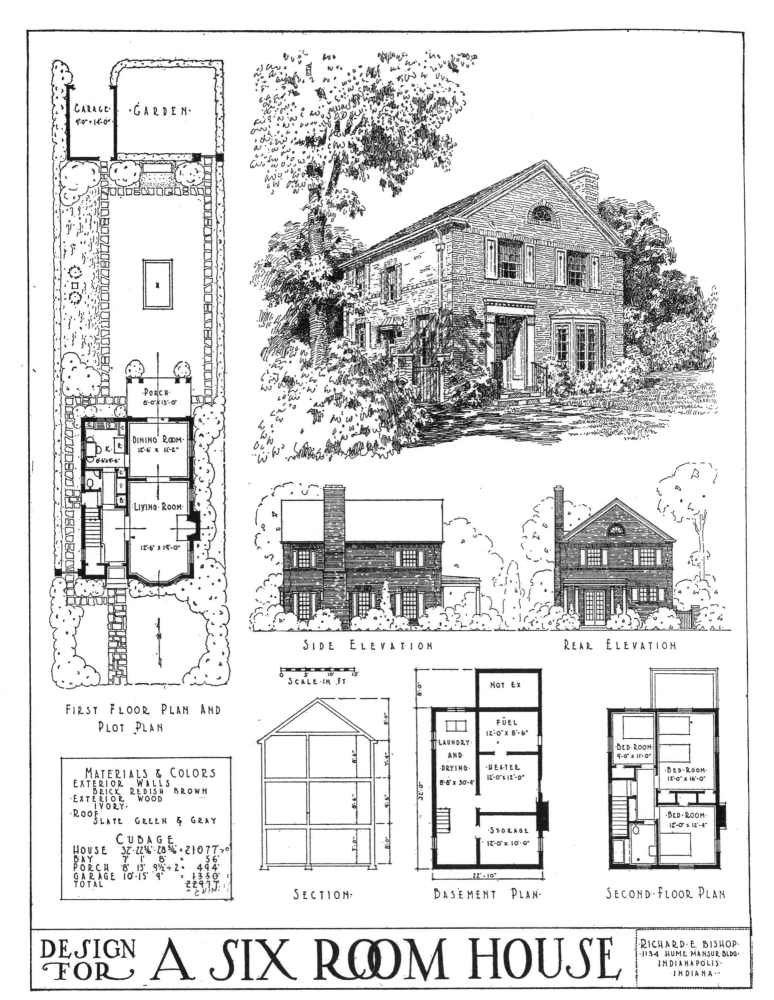

GARAGE
9'-0" × 14'-0"

·GARDEN·

PORCH
8'-0" × 13'-0"

DINING ROOM
12'-6" × 11'-2"

K. R.
8'-6" × 9'-6"

LIVING ROOM
12'-6" × 19'-0"

FIRST FLOOR PLAN AND
PLOT PLAN

MATERIALS & COLORS
EXTERIOR WALLS
    BRICK REDISH BROWN
EXTERIOR WOOD
    IVORY
ROOF
    SLATE GREEN & GRAY
CUBAGE
HOUSE 32'·22⅝'·28⅝' = 21077 ~0'
BAY   7'·1'·8'   =   56'
PORCH   8'·13'·9½÷2   =   494'
GARAGE 10'·15'·9'   = 1350'
TOTAL   22977.

SIDE ELEVATION

REAR ELEVATION

SCALE IN FT

SECTION

HOT EX

FUEL
12'-0" × 8'-6"

LAUNDRY
AND
DRYING
8'-6" × 30'-4"

HEATER
12'-0" × 12'-0"

STORAGE
12'-0" × 10'-0"

BASEMENT PLAN

BED ROOM
9'-0" × 11'-0"

BED ROOM
12'-0" × 16'-0"

BED ROOM
12'-0" × 12'-4"

SECOND FLOOR PLAN

DESIGN FOR A SIX ROOM HOUSE

RICHARD E. BISHOP
1134 HUME MANSUR BLDG.
INDIANAPOLIS
INDIANA

First Prize, Six Room House . . . RICHARD E. BISHOP, *Architect*

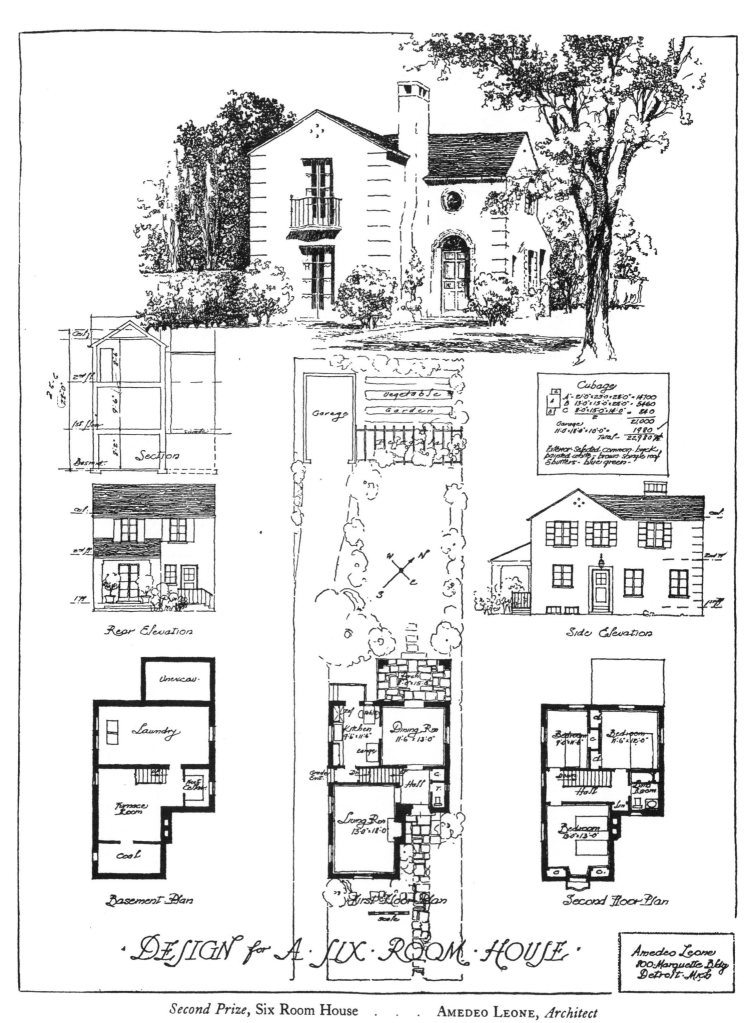

Section

Rear Elevation

Side Elevation

Cubage

A - 21'-0" x 25'-0" x 28'-0" = 14700
B - 13'-0" x 13'-0" x 28'-0" = 5460
C - 8'-0" x 15'-0" x 14'-0" = 840
                                 21000
Garage 11'-0" x 18'-0" x 10'-0" = 1980
                          Total - 22,980 ft

Exterior: Siding common brick,
painted white - brown shingle roof
& shutters - blue green.

Vegetable Garden

Garage

Basement Plan

American
Laundry
Furnace Room
coal

First Floor Plan

Kitchen 9'-6" x 11'-6"
Dining Rm 11'-6" x 13'-0"
Living Rm 13'-0" x 18'-0"
Hall
Porch

Second Floor Plan

Bedroom
Bedroom 11'-6" x 12'-0"
Hall
Bedroom 13'-0" x 13'-0"

·DESIGN for A·SIX·ROOM·HOUSE·

Amedeo Leone
800 Marquette Bldg
Detroit · Mich

Second Prize, Six Room House   .   .   .   Amedeo Leone, *Architect*

[22]

BASEMENT PLAN

SECOND FLOOR PLAN

REAR ELEVATION

SUBMITTED BY
LOUIS C. ROSENBERG AND
G. DEWEY SWAN
122 EAST 41ST STREET
NEW YORK CITY

DESIGN FOR A SIX-ROOM HOUSE

SECTION

SIDE ELEVATION

FIRST FLOOR PLAN

Third Prize, Six Room House . . . Louis C. Rosenberg and G. Dewey Swan, *Architects*

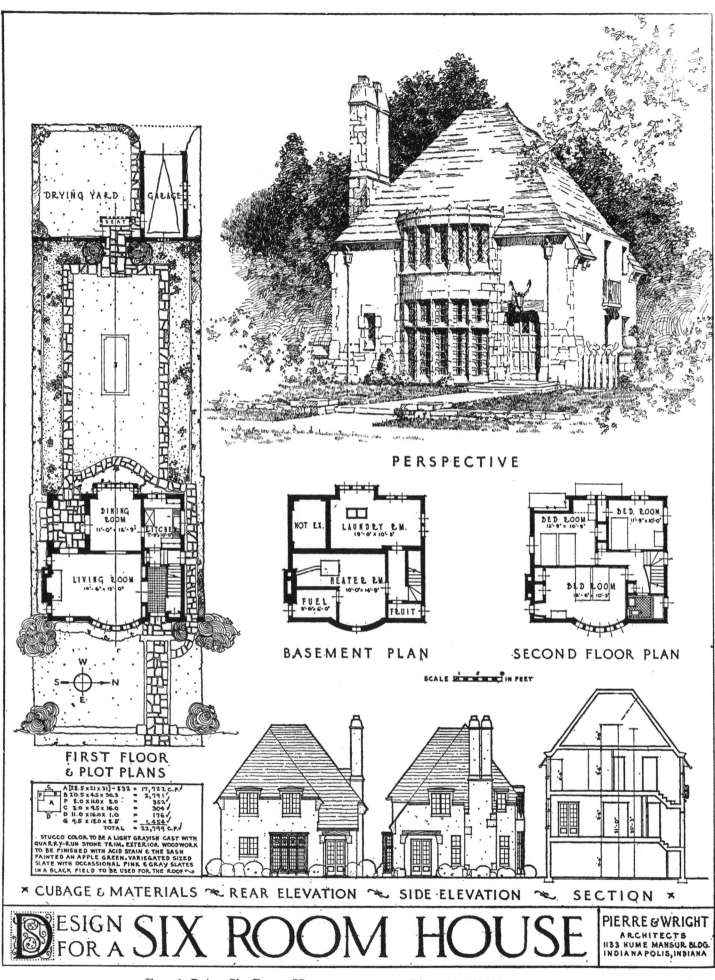

PERSPECTIVE

BASEMENT PLAN

SECOND FLOOR PLAN

SCALE IN FEET

FIRST FLOOR
& PLOT PLANS

STUCCO COLOR TO BE A LIGHT GRAYISH CAST WITH
QUARRY-RUN STONE TRIM. EXTERIOR WOODWORK
TO BE FINISHED WITH ACID STAIN & THE SASH
PAINTED AN APPLE GREEN. VARIEGATED SIZED
SLATE WITH OCCASSIONAL PINK & GRAY SLATES
IN A BLACK FIELD TO BE USED FOR THE ROOF

✕ CUBAGE & MATERIALS ⚜ REAR ELEVATION ⚜ SIDE ELEVATION ⚜ SECTION ✕

DESIGN SIX ROOM HOUSE
FOR A

PIERRE & WRIGHT
ARCHITECTS
1133 HUME MANSUR BLDG.
INDIANAPOLIS, INDIANA

Fourth Prize, Six Room House . . . Pierre & Wright, *Architects*

CUBAGE

L RM & WING 16'6"×28'6"×24'6" = 11679
D·RM · 14'6"×18'×27'5' = 7227
GARAGE · 19 × 10 × 18 = 3420
PORCH 6 × 18 × 8 × ½ = 432
CHIMNEY 4×2×6×8 = 80
DORMERS 3 @ 40 = 120
TOTAL 22958

NOTES

WALLS ·OF·BRICK WHITEWASHED
SHINGLE TILE ROOF ·OF·
VARIGATED COLORS WITH
WOODWORK A GRAY GREEN
STONE FLAG PAVING.

POOL

DRIVE

GARAGE
8'6"·17'6

PORCH

COAL

FP LIVING ROOM
15'0"·18'0

REF

CUP

RANGE KITCHEN SINK
8'6"·10

HALL CL CUP

DINING ROOM
11·0"·13'0

SOUTH ELEVATION

WEST
ELEVATION

CL TRUNKS

BED ROOM
8'6"·12'0

6'0" 27'·6 8·6 24·8 5·8 17'·6

8·6 8·6 8'0

DINING ROOM LIVING ROOM GARAGE
7'0 SECTIONS

CL

CL BED ROOM
12'0"·15'6

CL

CL

CL BATH

BED ROOM
11·0·13'0

COAL

BOILER ROOM TOILET

CL LAUNDRY

CHILDRENS
ROOM

DESIGN
FOR A
SIX ROOM HOUSE

H·R·BISHOP
10 EAST 43 St·
NEW YORK CITY

Fifth Prize, Six Room House   .   .   .   H. R. Bishop, *Architect*

DESIGN FOR A SIX ROOM HOVSE

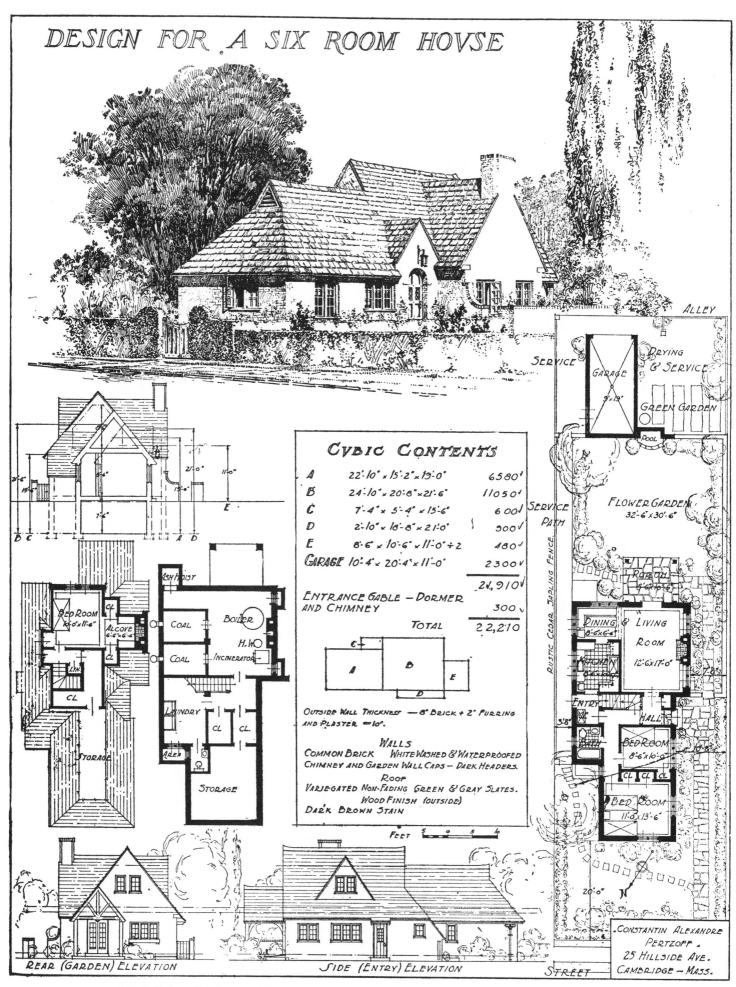

CVBIC CONTENTS

A	22'-10" × 15'-2" × 19'-0"	6580'
B	24'-10" × 20'-8" × 21'-6"	11050'
C	7'-4" × 5'-4" × 15'-6"	600'
D	2'-10" × 18'-8" × 21'-0"	900'
E	8'-6" × 10'-6" × 11'-0" ÷ 2	480'
GARAGE	10'-4" × 20'-4" × 11'-0"	2300'
		21,910'
ENTRANCE GABLE — DORMER AND CHIMNEY		300'
	TOTAL	22,210

OUTSIDE WALL THICKNESS — 8" BRICK + 2" FURRING
AND PLASTER = 10".

WALLS
COMMON BRICK   WHITE WASHED & WATERPROOFED
CHIMNEY AND GARDEN WALL CAPS — DARK HEADERS.

ROOF
VARIEGATED NON-FADING GREEN & GRAY SLATES.

WOOD FINISH (OUTSIDE)
DARK BROWN STAIN

FEET   5 0 5

REAR (GARDEN) ELEVATION   SIDE (ENTRY) ELEVATION   STREET

CONSTANTIN ALEXANDRE PERTZOFF.
25 HILLSIDE AVE.
CAMBRIDGE — MASS.

Sixth Prize, Six Room House   .   .   .   CONSTANTIN ALEXANDRE PERTZOFF, *Architect*

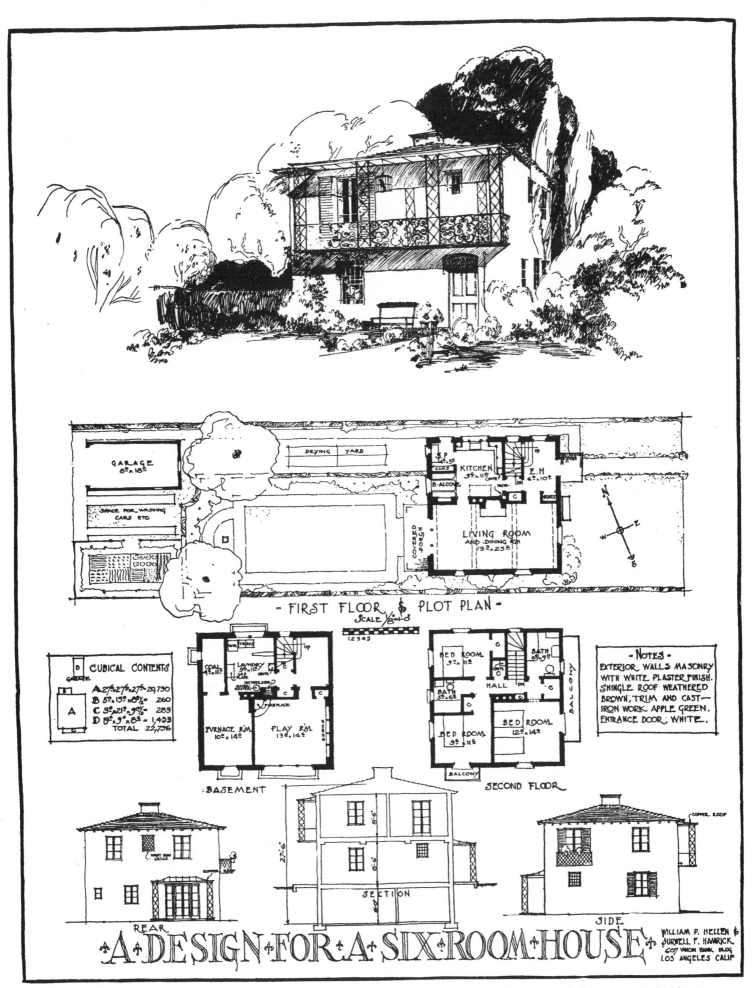

- FIRST FLOOR & PLOT PLAN -
SCALE ⅛"=1'0"

GARAGE
9ᵉ x 18ᵉ

SPACE FOR WASHING CARS ETC

DRYING YARD

S.P
KITCHEN
9ᵉ x 11ᵉ
CLOS
B. ALCOVE

E.H
6ᵉ x 10ᵉ

COVERED PORCH

LIVING ROOM
AND DINING RM
13ᵉ x 25ᵉ

CUBICAL CONTENTS
A 27ᵉ x 27ᵉ x 27ᵉ = 20,790
B 5ᵉ x 13ᵉ x 8½ = 260
C 3ᵉ x 21ᵉ x 9½ = 283
D 13ᵉ x 9ᵉ x 8½ = 1,433
TOTAL 22,736

GARAGE
A

COAL
4ᵉ x 11ᵉ
LAUNDRY
9ᵉ x 11ᵉ

HEATING

FURNACE RM
10ᵉ x 14ᵉ
PLAY RM
13ᵉ x 14ᵉ

BASEMENT

BED ROOM
9ᵉ x 11ᵉ
BATH
5ᵉ x 9ᵉ
BATH
5½ x 6ᵉ
HALL

BED ROOM
9ᵉ x 11ᵉ
BED ROOM
12ᵉ x 14ᵉ

BALCONY

BALCONY

SECOND FLOOR

- NOTES -
EXTERIOR WALLS MASONRY WITH WHITE PLASTER FINISH. SHINGLE ROOF WEATHERED BROWN; TRIM AND CAST-IRON WORK APPLE GREEN. ENTRANCE DOOR; WHITE.

WROT IRON GRILLE

REAR

27'-6"

SECTION

COPPER ROOF

SIDE

WILLIAM P. HELLEN &
BURWELL F. HAMRICK
607 UNION BANK BLDG
LOS ANGELES CALIF

A · DESIGN · FOR · A · SIX · ROOM · HOUSE

Seventh Prize, Six Room House . . . WILLIAM P. HELLEN AND BURWELL F. HAMRICK, *Architects*

[27]

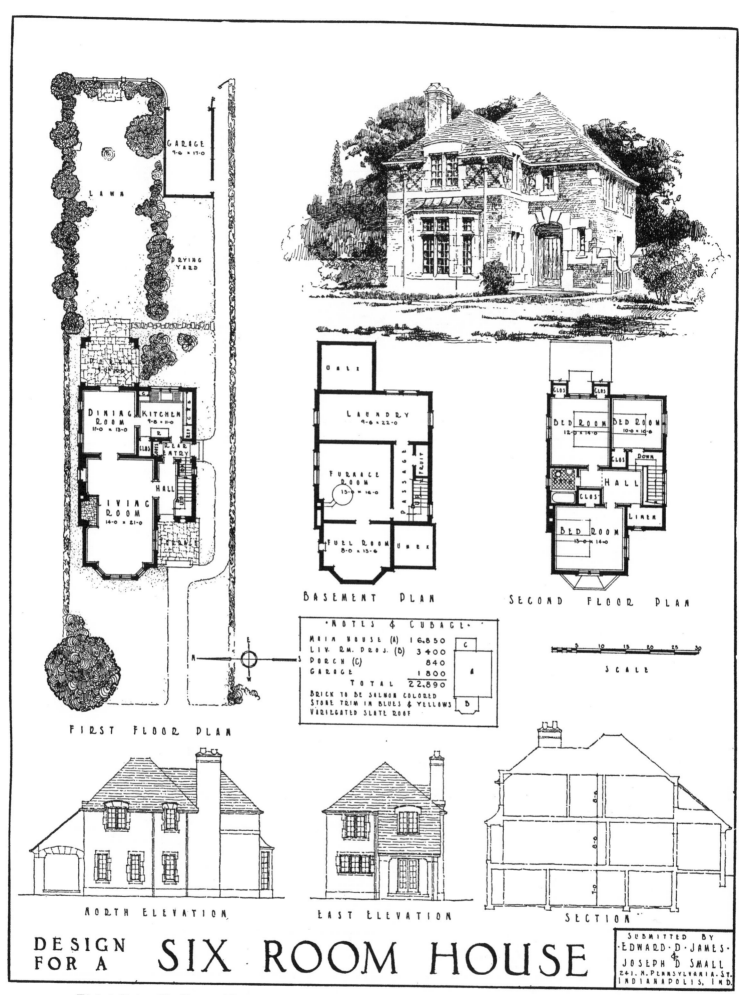

GARAGE
9-6 x 17-0

LAWN

DRYING
YARD

GARDEN
SHADE

DINING
ROOM
17-0 x 13-0

KITCHEN
9-8 x 11-0

REAR
ENTRY

HALL

LIVING
ROOM
14-0 x 21-0

FIRST FLOOR PLAN

WALK

LAUNDRY
9-6 x 22-0

FURNACE
ROOM
15-0 x 14-0

PASSAGE

FRUIT

FUEL ROOM
8-0 x 13-6

AREA

BASEMENT PLAN

CLOS CLOS

BED ROOM
12-0 x 14-0

BED ROOM
10-0 x 16-8

DOWN

CLOS

HALL

CLOS

LINEN

BED ROOM
13-0 x 14-0

SECOND FLOOR PLAN

·NOTES & CUBAGE·
MAIN HOUSE (A) 16,850
LIV. RM. PROJ. (B) 3,400
PORCH (C) 840
GARAGE 1,800
TOTAL 22,890
BRICK TO BE SALMON COLORED
STONE TRIM IN BLUES & YELLOWS
VARIEGATED SLATE ROOF

C
A
B

5 10 15 20 25 30
SCALE

NORTH ELEVATION

EAST ELEVATION

SECTION

DESIGN FOR A SIX ROOM HOUSE

SUBMITTED BY
·EDWARD·D·JAMES·
·JOSEPH·D·SMALL·
241. N. PENNSYLVANIA. ST.
INDIANAPOLIS. IND.

Eighth Prize, Six Room House . . . EDWARD D. JAMES AND JOSEPH D. SMALL, *Architects*

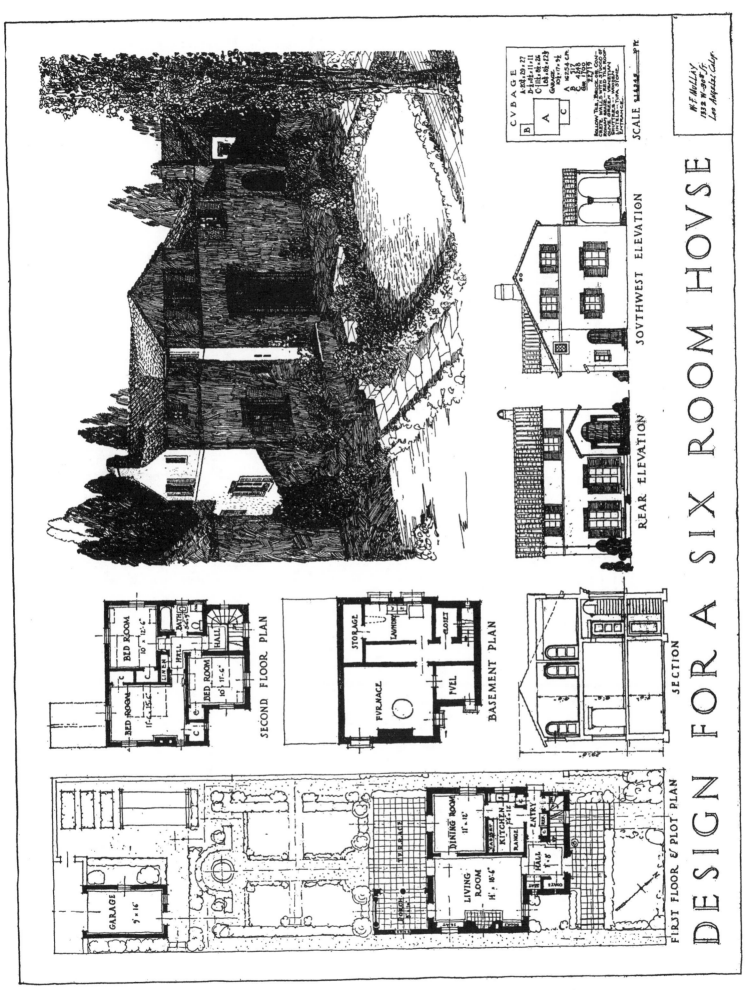

DESIGN FOR A SIX ROOM HOUSE

SOUTHWEST ELEVATION

REAR ELEVATION

SECOND FLOOR PLAN

BED ROOM
10'-0" x 12'-6"

BED ROOM
11'-5" x 15'-0"

BED ROOM
10'-0" x 11'-6"

BATH
5'x5'

HALL

BASEMENT PLAN

STORAGE

LAUNDRY

CLOSET

FURNACE

FUEL

SECTION

FIRST FLOOR & PLOT PLAN

GARAGE
9' x 16'

LIVING ROOM
14'-0" x 16'-6"

DINING ROOM
11' x 12'

KITCHEN
12' x 12'

TERRACE

PORCH

HALL

ENTRY

C V B A G E

Ninth Prize, Six Room House   .   .   .   W. F. MULLAY, *Architect*

[29]

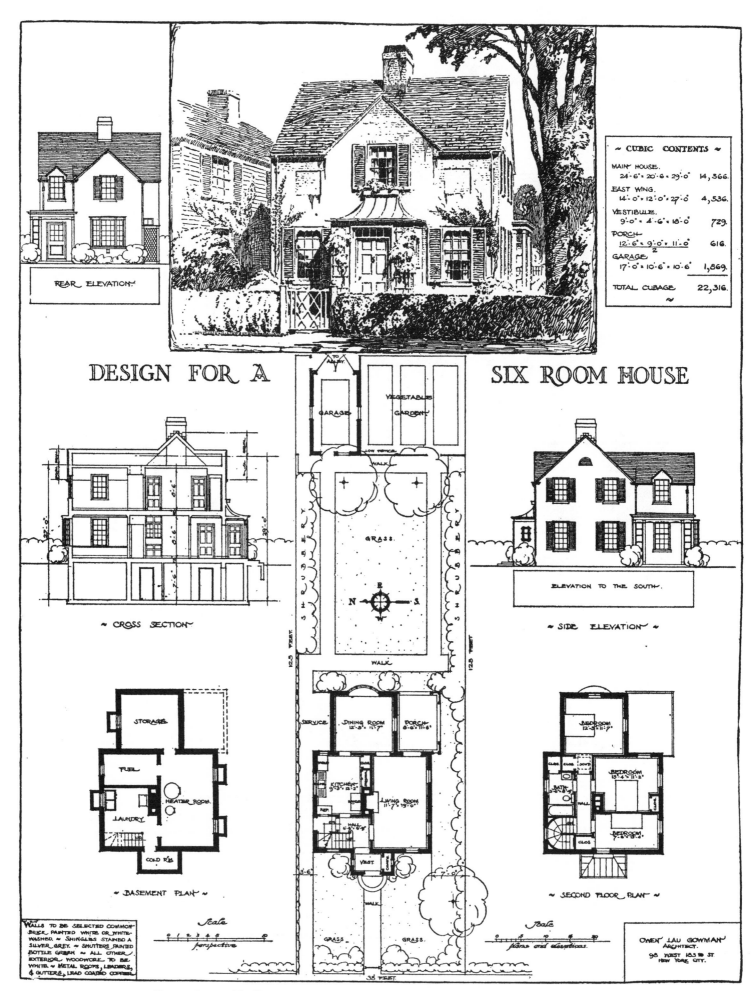

DESIGN FOR A   SIX ROOM HOUSE

REAR ELEVATION

~ CUBIC CONTENTS ~

MAIN HOUSE.
24'-6" x 20'-6" x 29'-0"   14,366.

EAST WING.
14'-0" x 12'-0" x 27'-0"   4,536.

VESTIBULE.
9'-0" x 4'-6" x 18'-0"   729.

PORCH.
12'-6" x 9'-0" x 11'-0" / 2   616.

GARAGE.
17'-0" x 10'-6" x 10'-6"   1,869.

TOTAL CUBAGE   22,316.

~ CROSS SECTION ~

ELEVATION TO THE SOUTH.

~ SIDE ELEVATION ~

~ BASEMENT PLAN ~

~ SECOND FLOOR PLAN ~

WALLS TO BE SELECTED COMMON BRICK, PAINTED WHITE OR WHITE-WASHED. ~ SHINGLES STAINED A SILVER-GREY. ~ SHUTTERS PAINTED BOTTLE GREEN ~ ALL OTHER EXTERIOR WOODWORK TO BE WHITE ~ METAL ROOFS, LEADERS, & GUTTERS, LEAD COATED COPPER.

Scale
perspective

Scale
plans and elevations.

OWEN LAU GOWMAN
ARCHITECT.
98 WEST 183 ST.
NEW YORK CITY.

Tenth Prize, Six Room House   .   .   .   Owen Lau Gowman, *Architect*

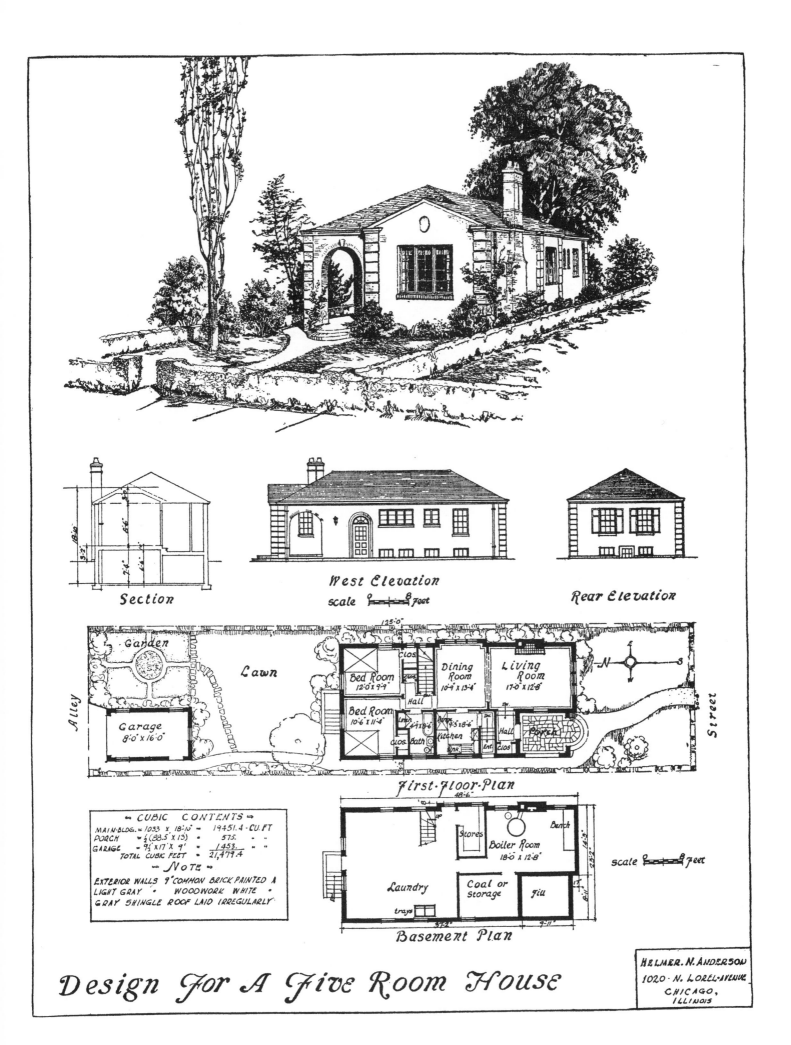

Section

West Elevation
scale 0___8 feet

Rear Elevation

Garden

Lawn

Alley

Garage
8'-0" x 16'-0"

Bed Room
12'-0" x 9'-9"

Bed Room
10'-6" x 11'-4"

Clos.

Clos.

Hall

Linen
4'-1"x9'-6"

Clos.

Bath

Kitchen

Dining
Room
10'-9" x 13'-4"

Living
Room
17'-0" x 12'-6"

Pantry
9'-5"x8'-6"

Ent.

Hall

Clos.

Porch

N

S

Street

125'-0"

First Floor Plan

CUBIC CONTENTS
MAIN·BLDG.= 1033 X 18'-10" = 19451.4 CU.FT
PORCH = ½ (88.5 X 13) = 575. " "
GARAGE = 9½' X 17' X 9' = 1453. " "
TOTAL CUBIC FEET = 21,479.4
NOTE
EXTERIOR WALLS 9" COMMON BRICK PAINTED A
LIGHT GRAY · WOODWORK WHITE ·
GRAY SHINGLE ROOF LAID IRREGULARLY

48'-6"

Stores

Boiler Room
18'-0" x 12'-8"

Bench

Laundry

Coal or
Storage

Flu

trays

37'-2"

9'-11"

Basement Plan

scale 0___8 feet

Design For A Five Room House

HELMER. N. ANDERSON
1020 · N. LOREL·AVENUE
CHICAGO,
ILLINOIS

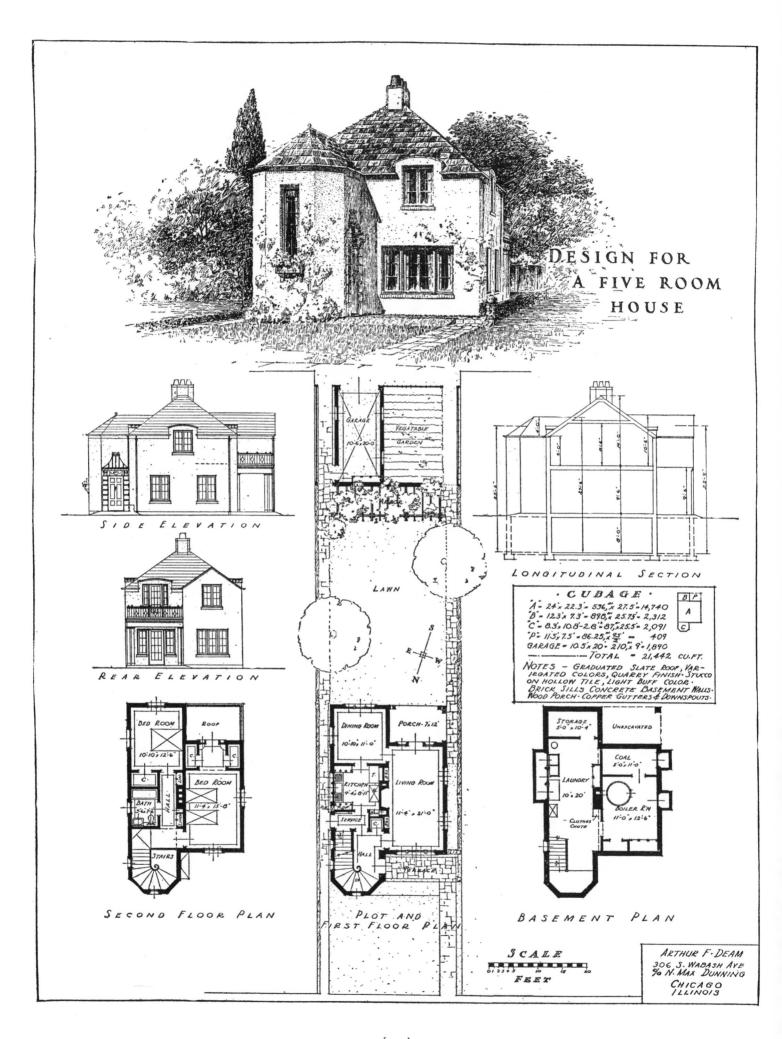

DESIGN FOR
A FIVE ROOM
HOUSE

SIDE ELEVATION

REAR ELEVATION

SECOND FLOOR PLAN

LONGITUDINAL SECTION

PLOT AND
FIRST FLOOR PLAN

BASEMENT PLAN

· CUBAGE ·
A = 24' x 22.3 = 536.' x 27.5' = 14,740
B = 12.3' x 7.3' = 898.' x 25.75 = 2,312
C = 8.3' x 10.8 - 2.8' = 87.' x 25.5 = 2,091
P = 11.5' x 7.5' = 86.25.' x 9.5' = 409
GARAGE = 10.5 x 20 = 210.' x 9 = 1,890
——— TOTAL = 21,442 CU.FT.
NOTES - GRADUATED SLATE ROOF, VAR-
IEGATED COLORS, QUARRY FINISH · STUCCO
ON HOLLOW TILE, LIGHT BUFF COLOR ·
BRICK SILLS · CONCRETE BASEMENT WALLS ·
WOOD PORCH · COPPER GUTTERS & DOWNSPOUTS.

SCALE
FEET

ARTHUR F· DEAM
306 S. WABASH AVE
℅ N· MAX DUNNING
CHICAGO
ILLINOIS

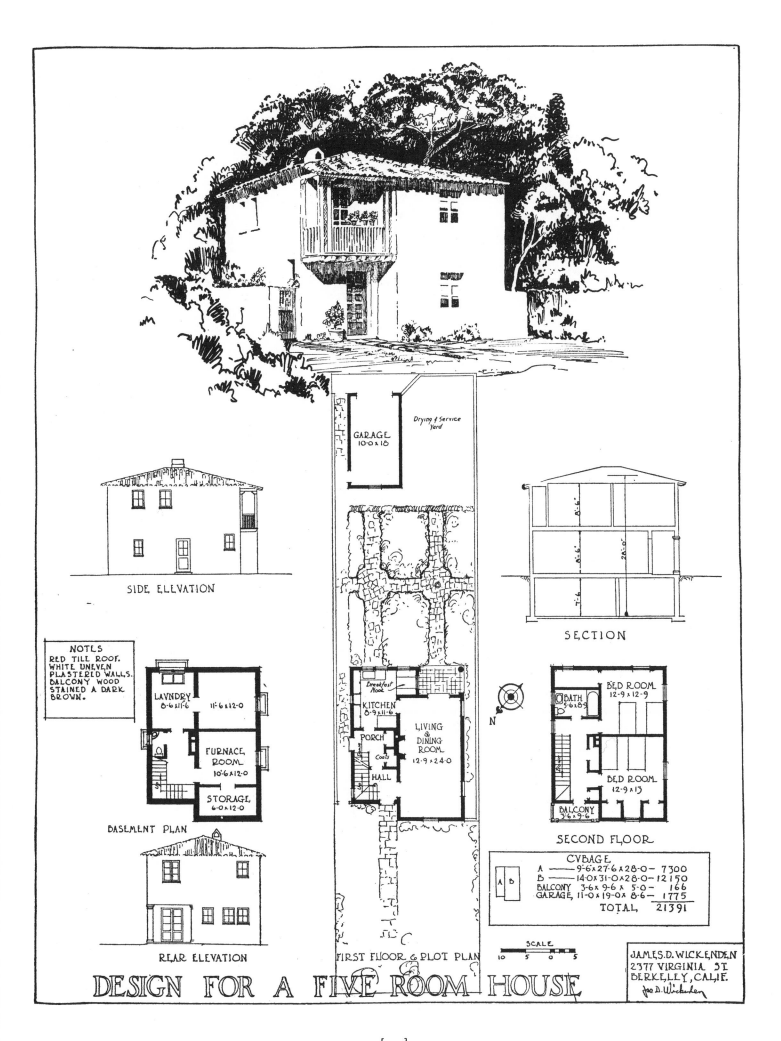

SIDE ELEVATION

NOTES
RED TILE ROOF.
WHITE UNEVEN
PLASTERED WALLS.
BALCONY WOOD
STAINED A DARK
BROWN.

GARAGE
10-0 x 18

Drying & Service
Yard

SECTION

8-6

10-6

7-6

26-0

LAVNDRY
8-6 x 11-6   11-6 x 12-0

FURNACE
ROOM
10-6 x 12-0

STORAGE
6-0 x 12-0

BASEMENT PLAN

Breakfast
Nook

KITCHEN
8-9 x 11-6

PORCH

Coals

HALL

LIVING
&
DINING
ROOM
12-9 x 24-0

N

BATH
5-6 x 8-9

BED ROOM
12-9 x 12-9

BED ROOM
12-9 x 13

BALCONY
3-6 x 9-6

SECOND FLOOR

CVBAGE
A ——— 9-6 x 27-6 x 28-0 — 7300
B ——— 14-0 x 31-0 x 28-0 — 12150
BALCONY 3-6 x 9-6 x 5-0 — 166
GARAGE 11-0 x 19-0 x 8-6 — 1775
TOTAL 21391

A B

REAR ELEVATION

FIRST FLOOR & PLOT PLAN

SCALE
10 5 0 5

JAMES D. WICKENDEN
2377 VIRGINIA ST
BERKELEY, CALIF.
Jas D. Wickenden

DESIGN FOR A FIVE ROOM HOUSE

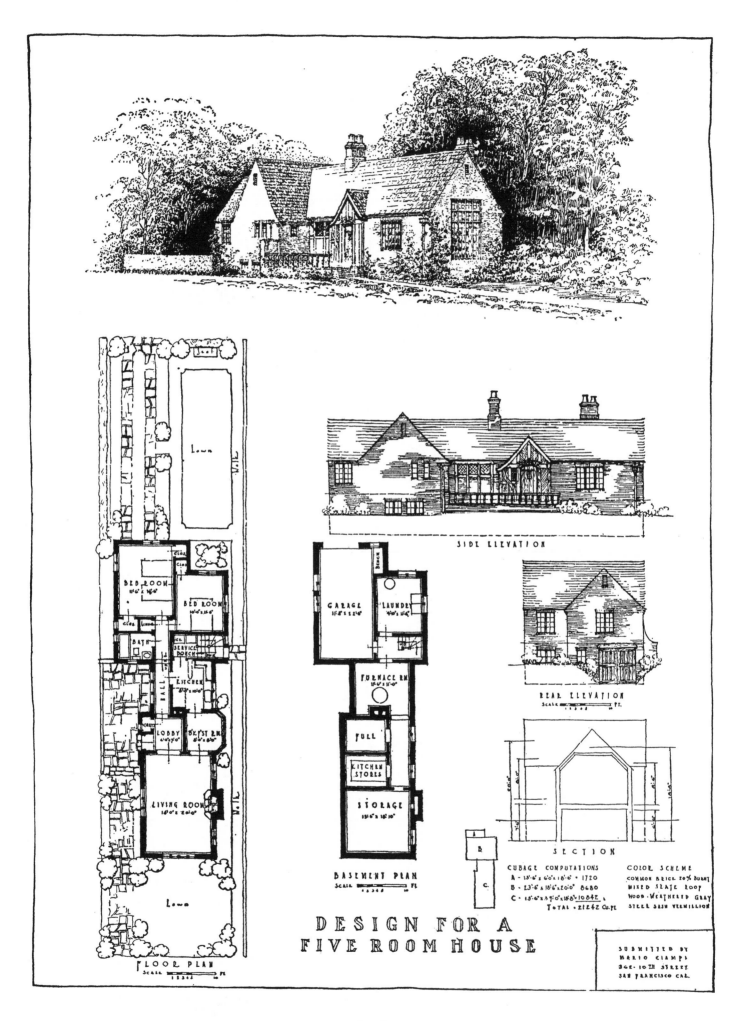

SIDE ELEVATION

REAR ELEVATION
Scale ____ FT.

BED ROOM
16'-6" x 16'-0"

BED ROOM
10'-0" x 15'-0"

BATH

SERVICE PORCH

KITCHEN
8'-0" x 10'-0"

LOBBY
7'-0" x 8'-0"

BKF'ST RM
8'-0" x 8'-0"

LIVING ROOM
16'-0" x 20'-0"

Lawn

HALL

Lawn

FLOOR PLAN
SCALE ____ FT.

GARAGE
11'-8" x 21'-0"

LAUNDRY
9'-0" x 14'-0"

FURNACE RM
16'-0" x 11'-0"

FULL

KITCHEN STORES

STORAGE
13'-6" x 16'-10"

BASEMENT PLAN
Scale ____ FT.

SECTION

A
B
C

CUBAGE COMPUTATIONS
A - 13'-6" x 60'-0" x 16'-6" = 1720
B - 23'-6" x 16'-6" x 20'-0" = 8680
C - 13'-6" x 37'-0" x 15'-8" = 10842
Total = 21242 Cu.Ft.

COLOR SCHEME
COMMON BRICK 20% BURNT
MIXED SLATE ROOF
WOOD - WEATHERED GRAY
STEEL SASH VERMILLION

DESIGN FOR A FIVE ROOM HOUSE

SUBMITTED BY
MARIO CIAMPI
342 - 10TH STREET
SAN FRANCISCO CAL.

DESIGN FOR A FIVE ROOM HOUSE

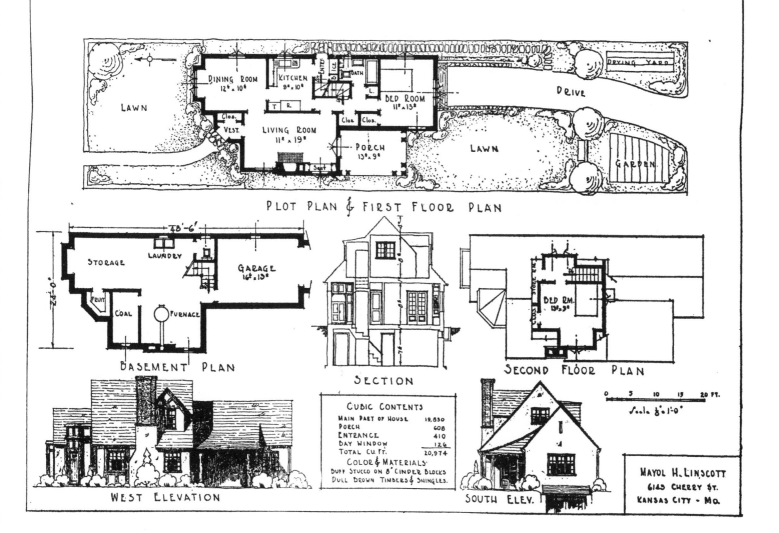

PLOT PLAN & FIRST FLOOR PLAN

Plot/First Floor Plan labels:
LAWN · DINING ROOM 12'×10' · KITCHEN 9'×10' · BATH · BED ROOM 11'×13' · DRYING YARD · DRIVE · VEST. · LIVING ROOM 11'×19' · Clos. · Clos. · Clos. · PORCH 13'×9' · LAWN · GARDEN

Basement Plan labels:
STORAGE · LAUNDRY · GARAGE 16'×19' · FRUIT · COAL · FURNACE · 48'-6' · 22'-0"

BASEMENT PLAN

SECTION

BED RM. 13'×9'

SECOND FLOOR PLAN

WEST ELEVATION

CUBIC CONTENTS
MAIN PART OF HOUSE 19,830
PORCH 608
ENTRANCE 410
DAY WINDOW 126
TOTAL CU. FT. 20,974
COLOR & MATERIALS:
BUFF STUCCO ON 8" CINDER BLOCKS
DULL BROWN TIMBERS & SHINGLES.

SOUTH ELEV.

0   5   10   15   20 FT.
Scale ⅛"=1'-0"

MAYOL H. LINSCOTT
6143 CHERRY ST.
KANSAS CITY · MO.

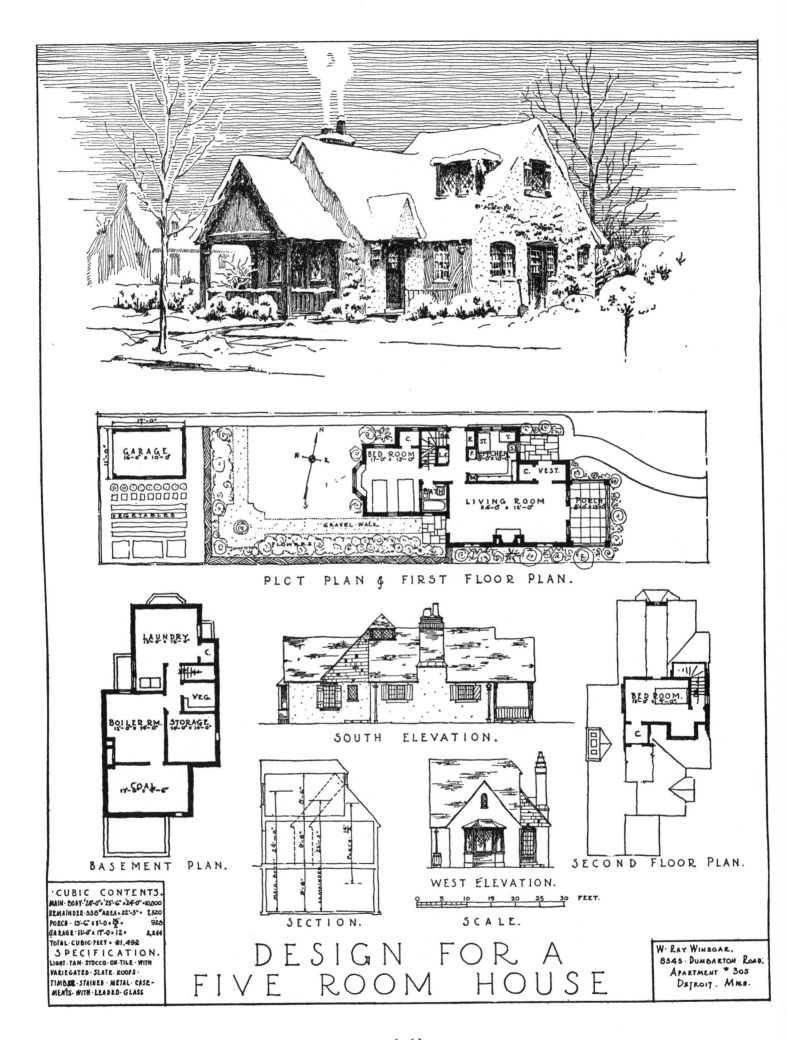

PLOT PLAN & FIRST FLOOR PLAN.

GARAGE
16'-0" x 10'-0"

VEGETABLES

BED ROOM
17'-0" x 13'-0"

BATH

KITCHEN
8'-0" x 10'-0"

C. VEST.

LIVING ROOM
24'-0" x 12'-0"

PORCH

GRAVEL WALK

FLOWERS

BASEMENT PLAN.

LAUNDRY

C.

VEG.

BOILER RM.
12'-0" x 14'-0"

STORAGE
16'-0" x 10'-0"

SOUTH ELEVATION.

SECTION.

WEST ELEVATION.

SCALE.

0   5   10   15   20   25   30   FEET.

SECOND FLOOR PLAN.

BED ROOM
16'-0" x 12'-0"

C.

CUBIC CONTENTS.
MAIN·BODY·24'-0"×25'-6"×24'-0" = 10,800
REMAINDER·338"AREA×22'-3" = 7,520
PORCH·15'-6"×8'-0"× ½ = 928
GARAGE·11'-0"×17'-0"×12 = 2,244
TOTAL·CUBIC·FEET = 21,492
SPECIFICATION.
LIGHT·TAN·STUCCO·ON·TILE·WITH
VARIEGATED·SLATE·ROOFS
TIMBER·STAINED·METAL·CASE-
MENTS·WITH·LEADED·GLASS

DESIGN FOR A
FIVE ROOM HOUSE

W·RAY·WINEGAR.
8545·DUMBARTON·ROAD;
APARTMENT # 305
DETROIT. MICH.

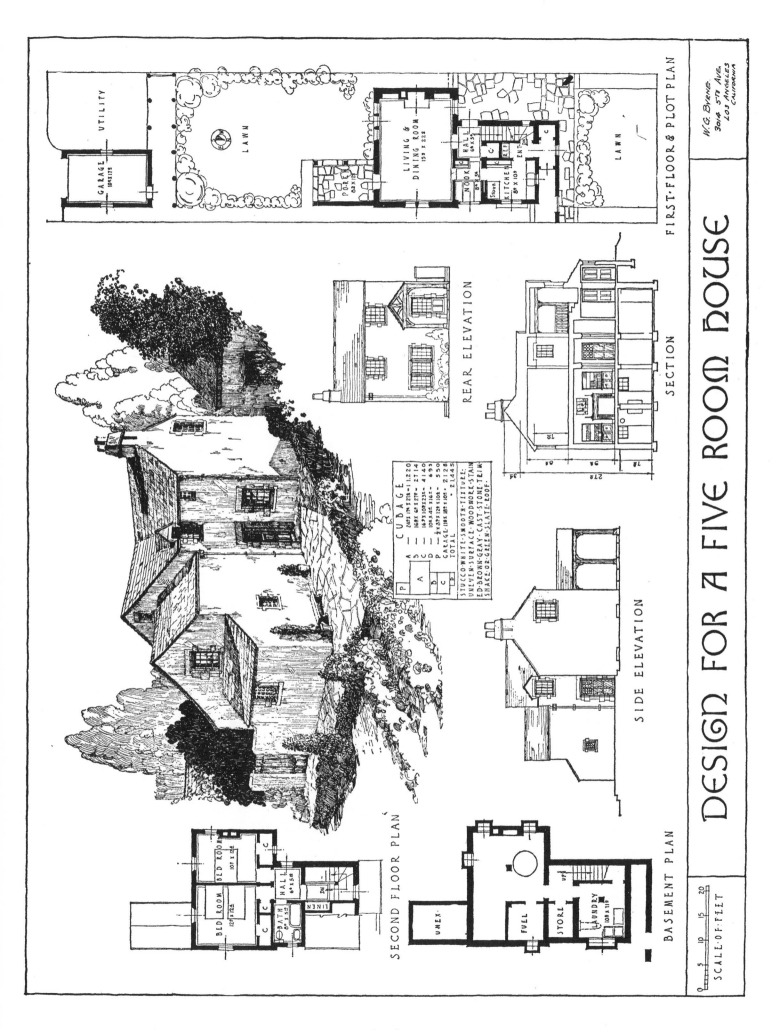

FIRST·FLOOR·&·PLOT·PLAN

GARAGE
10⁵x17⁵

UTILITY

LAWN

LIVING &
DINING ROOM
15⁹ x 22⁵

NOOK
8⁵ x 5⁵

HALL
6⁹ x 3⁵

P·O·R·
6⁵ x 11⁵

REF·

STOVE·

KITCHEN
8⁵ x 10⁵

LAWN

REAR ELEVATION

SECTION

CUBAGE	
A — 24⁹·1¹¹x 17⁷⁸ =	11,220
B — 16⁸x 6¹x 27¹² =	2714
C — 16⁷x 10⁸x 23⁸=	4140
D — 10⁴x 4⁴x 16⁷ =	693
P — ⁸⁄₄x 37¹x 12⁴x 10⁸=	550
GARAGE·10⁵x 18⁵x 10⁸·	2128
TOTAL	·21,445

STUCCO·WHITE·SMOOTH·TEXTURE·
UNEVEN·SURFACE·WOODWORK·STAIN-
ED·BROWN·GRAY·CAST·STONE·TRIM·
SHAKE·OR·GREEN·SLATE·ROOF·

SIDE ELEVATION

BED ROOM
10⁵ x 12⁸

BED ROOM
12⁸ x 17⁵

BATH
6⁵ x 5⁵

HALL
6⁸ x 15⁸

LINEN

SECOND FLOOR PLAN

UNEX·

FUEL

STORE

LAUNDRY
10⁸ x 11⁹

UP

BASEMENT PLAN

DESIGN FOR A FIVE ROOM HOUSE

W.G. BYRNE·
3014 5ᵀᴴ AVE·
LOS ANGELES
CALIFORNIA

0 5 10 15 20
SCALE·OF·FEET

FIRST FLOOR and PLOT PLAN

REAR ELEVATION

SIDE ELEVATION

GRAPHIC SCALE

SECOND FLOOR PLAN

BASEMENT PLAN

SECTION

DESIGN FOR A FIVE ROOM HOUSE

R. Van Deren Livingston
3132 Carlyle St.
Los Angeles.
California.

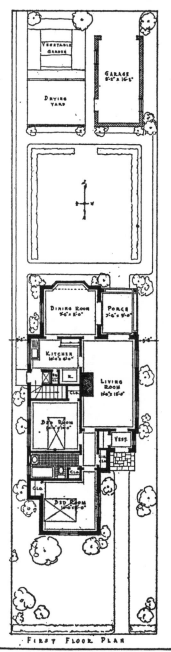

FIRST FLOOR PLAN

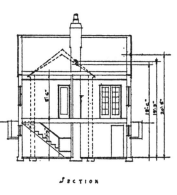

WEST ELEVATION

SECTION

SOUTH ELEVATION

A	15'-8" x 10'-0" x 18'-6"	2249
Bay	5'-0" x 1'-6" x 15'-0"	132
B	½(7'-6" x 5'-0" x 10'-0")	530
C	25'-6" x 19'-6" x 18'-9"	9779
D	2'-6" x 10'-6"	56
E	17'-6" x 26'-6"	464
F	7'-6" x 4'-0"	90
G	2'-6" x 4'-0"	60
	582 x 15'-6"	6991
Garage 10'-0" x 18'-0" x 10'-0"		1800
	TOTAL	20679 CU. FT.

WALLS - ROUGH TEXTURED WHITE STUCCO
ROOF - BROWN STAINED SHINGLES
EXTERIOR WOODWORK - STAINED BROWN
SASH - CASEMENT TYPE

BASEMENT PLAN

DESIGN FOR A
FIVE ROOM HOUSE

CLARENCE B. MACKAY &
AND GEORGE F. AXT

% CLARENCE B. MACKAY
538 CENTRAL AVE.
NEW HAVEN - CONN.

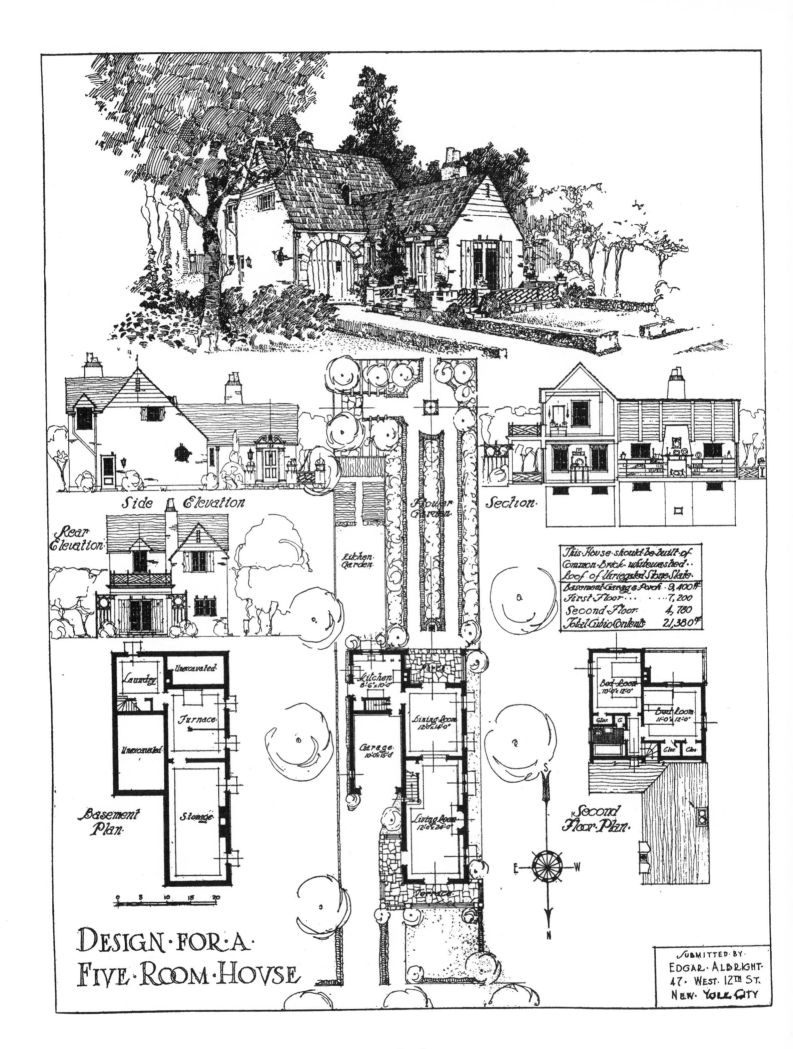

DESIGN·FOR·A·
FIVE·ROOM·HOVSE

Side Elevation

Rear Elevation

Flower Garden

Section

Kitchen Garden

This House should be built of
Common Brick whitewashed·
Roof of Variegated Shingle Slate.
Basement Garage & Porch 9,400#
First Floor · · · · · · 7,200
Second Floor 4,780
Total Cubic Contents 21,380#

Basement Plan.

Laundry Unexcavated
Furnace·
Unexcavated Storage.

Kitchen
8'-6"x10'-0"

Dining Room
12'-0"x14'-0"

Garage
10'-0"x15'-6"

Living Room
12'-0"x24'-0"

Terrace

Second Floor Plan.

Bed Room
10'-0"x12'-0"

Bed Room
11'-0"x12'-0"

SUBMITTED·BY·
EDGAR·ALBRIGHT·
47·WEST·12TH·ST·
NEW·YORK·CITY

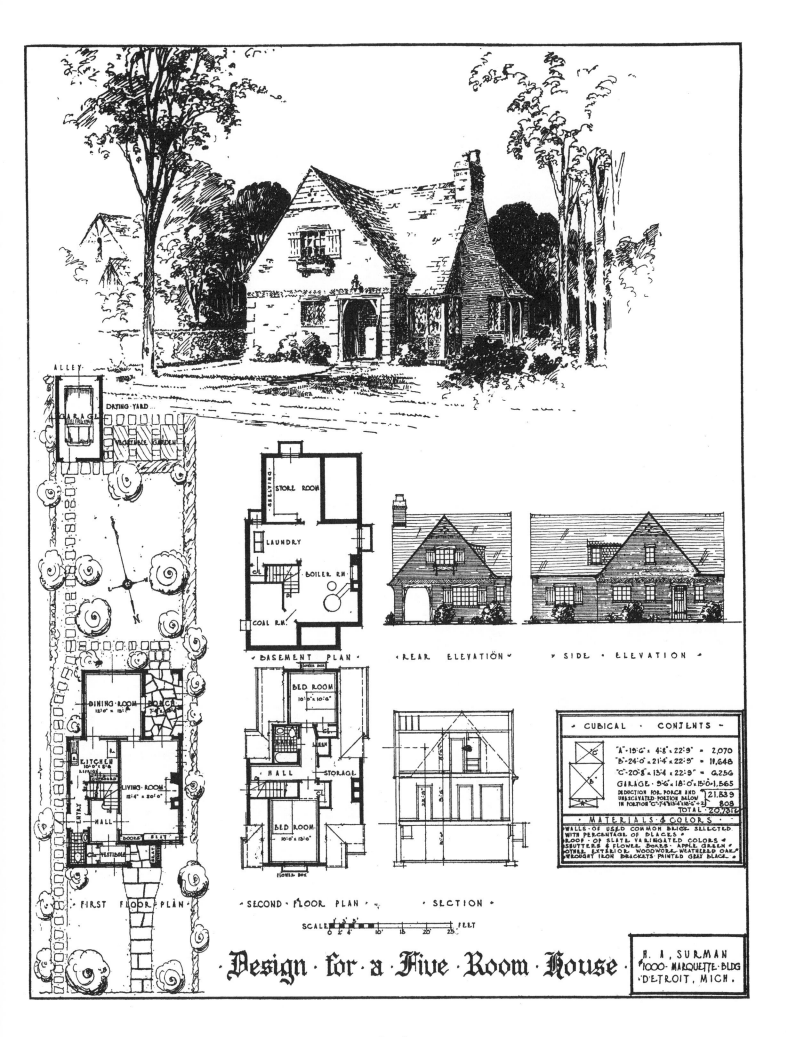

ALLEY

GARAGE

DRYING YARD

VEGETABLE GARDEN

N

DINING ROOM
13'-0" x 13'-0"

PORCH

KITCHEN
10'-0" x 8'-6"

LIVING ROOM
13'-4" x 20'-0"

HALL

ENTRY

VESTIBULE

· FIRST · FLOOR · PLAN ·

SHELVING

STORE ROOM

LAUNDRY

BOILER RM.

COAL RM.

· BASEMENT · PLAN ·

· SECOND · FLOOR · PLAN ·

BED ROOM
10'-0" x 10'-4"

HALL

STORAGE

BED ROOM
10'-0" x 13'-0"

FLOWER BOX

· REAR · ELEVATION ·

· SIDE · ELEVATION ·

· SECTION ·

SCALE   FEET
0 2 4   10   15   20   25

· CUBICAL · CONTENTS ·

"A" - 19'-6" x 4'-8" x 22'-9" = 2,070
"B" - 24'-0" x 21'-4" x 22'-9" = 11,648
"C" - 20'-8" x 13'-4" x 22'-9" = 6,256
GARAGE - 9'-6" x 18'-0" x 15'-0" = 1,565
DEDUCTION FOR PORCH AND
UNEXCAVATED PORTION BELOW
IN PORTION "C" - 7'-6" x 13'-4" x 18'-0" ÷ 2)   21,539
  808
TOTAL - 20,731

· MATERIALS · & · COLORS ·

WALLS OF USED COMMON BRICK SELECTED
WITH PERCENTAGE OF BLACKS ·
ROOF OF SLATE VARIEGATED COLORS ·
SHUTTERS & FLOWER BOXES · APPLE GREEN ·
OTHER EXTERIOR WOODWORK WEATHERED OAK ·
WROUGHT IRON BRACKETS PAINTED GREY BLACK ·

Design · for · a · Five · Room · House

H. A. SURMAN
1000 · MARQUETTE · BLDG
· DETROIT, MICH.

DESIGN FOR A FIVE ROOM HOUSE

ROBERT V. WADE &
FRED J. ABENDROTH
1969 EAST 82 ND ST
CLEVELAND OHIO

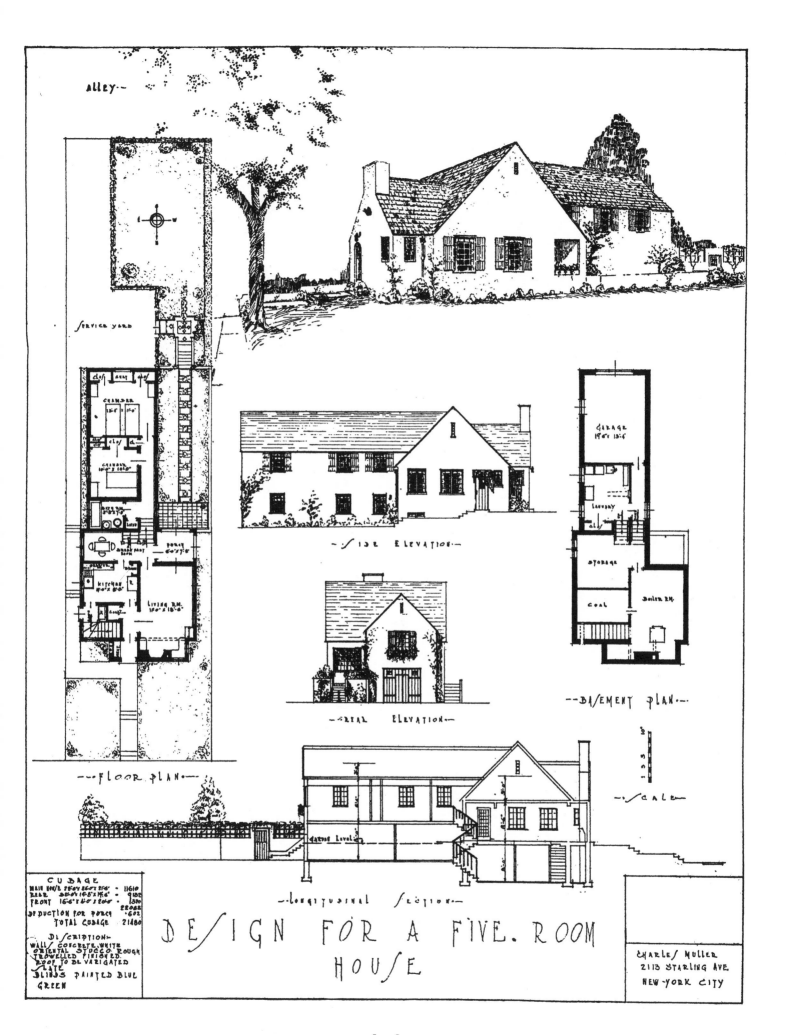

alley—

service yard

—FLOOR PLAN—

—SIDE ELEVATION—

—REAR ELEVATION—

—BASEMENT PLAN—

—SCALE—

—LONGITUDINAL SECTION—

CUBAGE

DESIGN FOR A FIVE-ROOM
HOUSE

CHARLES MULLER
2113 STARLING AVE.
NEW YORK CITY

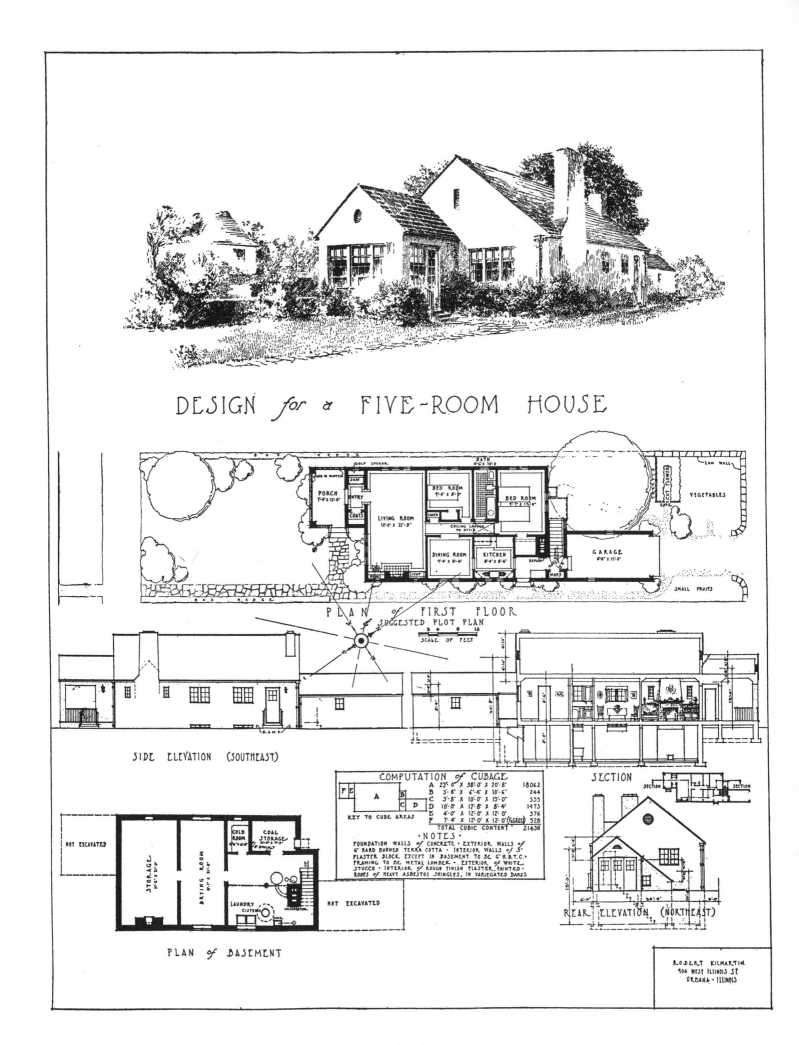

DESIGN for a FIVE-ROOM HOUSE

PLAN of FIRST FLOOR
SUGGESTED PLOT PLAN

SCALE OF FEET

SIDE ELEVATION (SOUTHEAST)

SECTION

COMPUTATION of CUBAGE

A	23'-0" X 38'-0" X 20'-8"	18062
B	3'-8" X 6'-4" X 10'-6"	244
C	3'-8" X 10'-0" X 15'-0"	555
D	10'-0" X 17'-8" X 8'-4"	1473
E	4'-0" X 12'-0" X 12'-0"	576
F	7'-4" X 12'-0" X 12'-0" (½ GROSS)	528
	TOTAL CUBIC CONTENT	21438

KEY TO CUBE AREAS

NOTES

FOUNDATION WALLS OF CONCRETE · EXTERIOR WALLS OF
6" HARD BURNED TERRA COTTA · INTERIOR WALLS OF 3"
PLASTER BLOCK EXCEPT IN BASEMENT TO BE 6" H.B.T.C.
FRAMING TO BE METAL LUMBER · EXTERIOR OF WHITE
STUCCO · INTERIOR OF ROUGH FINISH PLASTER, PAINTED
ROOFS OF HEAVY ASBESTOS SHINGLES, IN VARIEGATED DARES

PLAN of BASEMENT

REAR ELEVATION (NORTHEAST)

ROBERT KILMARTIN
904 WEST ILLINOIS ST
URBANA · ILLINOIS

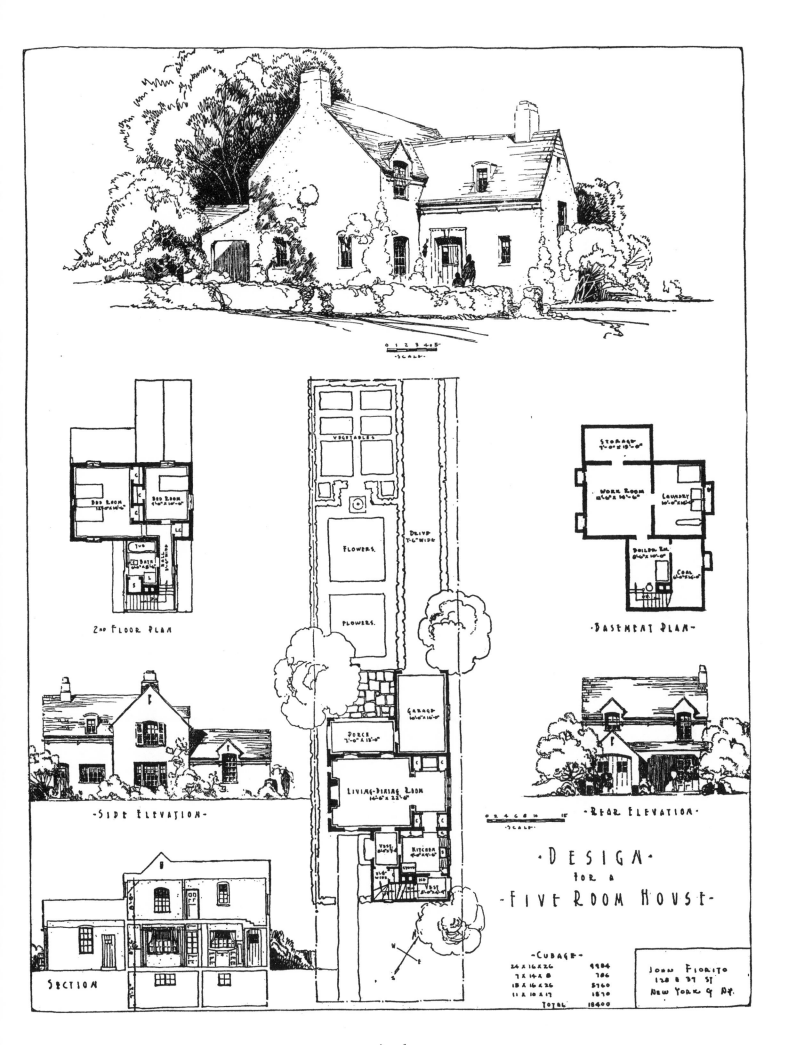

0 1 2 3 4 5
·SCALE·

2ND FLOOR PLAN

BED ROOM

BED ROOM
9'-0" X 16'-0"

BATH

VEGETABLES

FLOWERS.

DRIVE
7'-6" WIDE

FLOWERS.

STORAGE
7'-0" X 13'-0"

WORK ROOM
21'-6" X 10'-6"

LAUNDRY
10'-0" X 10'

BOILER RM.
8'-6" X 10'-0"

COAL

·BASEMENT PLAN·

·SIDE ELEVATION·

GARAGE
10'-0" X 16'-0"

PORCH
7'-0" X 13'-0"

LIVING-DINING ROOM
14'-6" X 22'-6"

VEST.

KITCHEN

0 2 4 6 8 10   15
·SCALE·

·REAR ELEVATION·

·DESIGN·
FOR A
·FIVE ROOM HOUSE·

SECTION

JOHN FIORITO
128 E 39 ST
NEW YORK 9 NY.

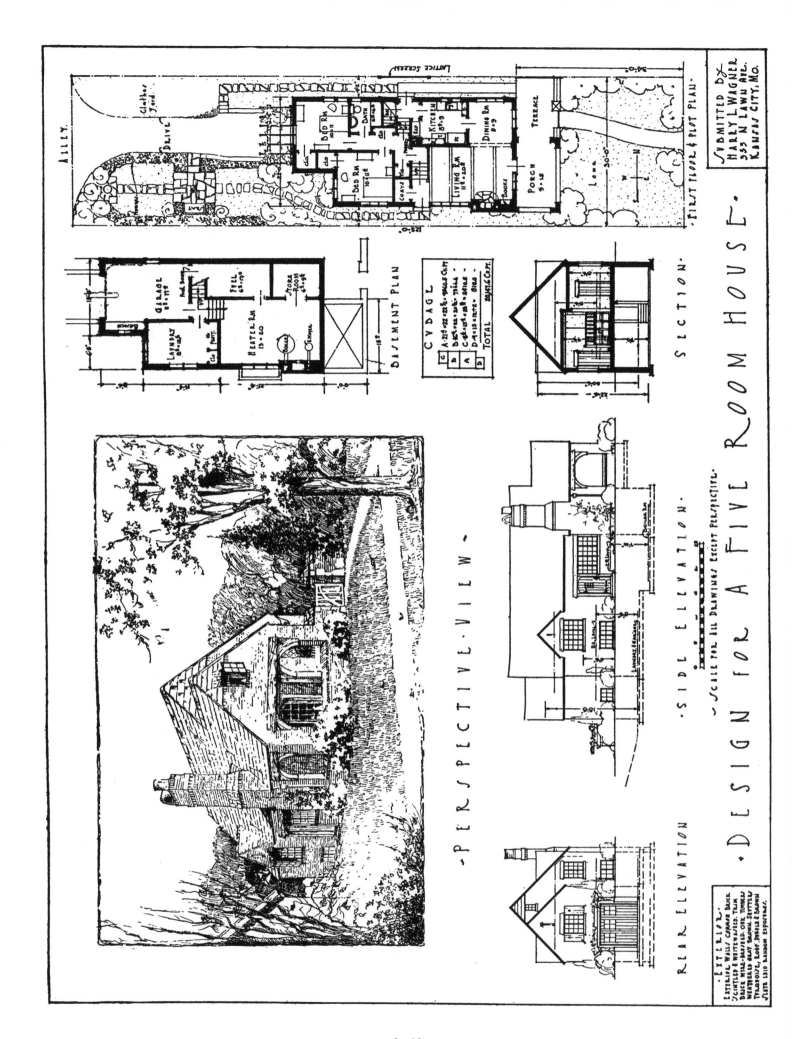

SUBMITTED BY
HARLEY L. WAGNER.
355 N LAWN AVE.
KANSAS CITY, MO.

• FIRST FLOOR & PLOT PLAN •

• BASEMENT PLAN •

CVBAGE

• PERSPECTIVE • VIEW •

• SECTION •

• SIDE • ELEVATION •

~ SCALE FOR ALL DRAWINGS EXCEPT PERSPECTIVE •

• REAR ELEVATION •

• DESIGN FOR A FIVE ROOM HOUSE •

[46]

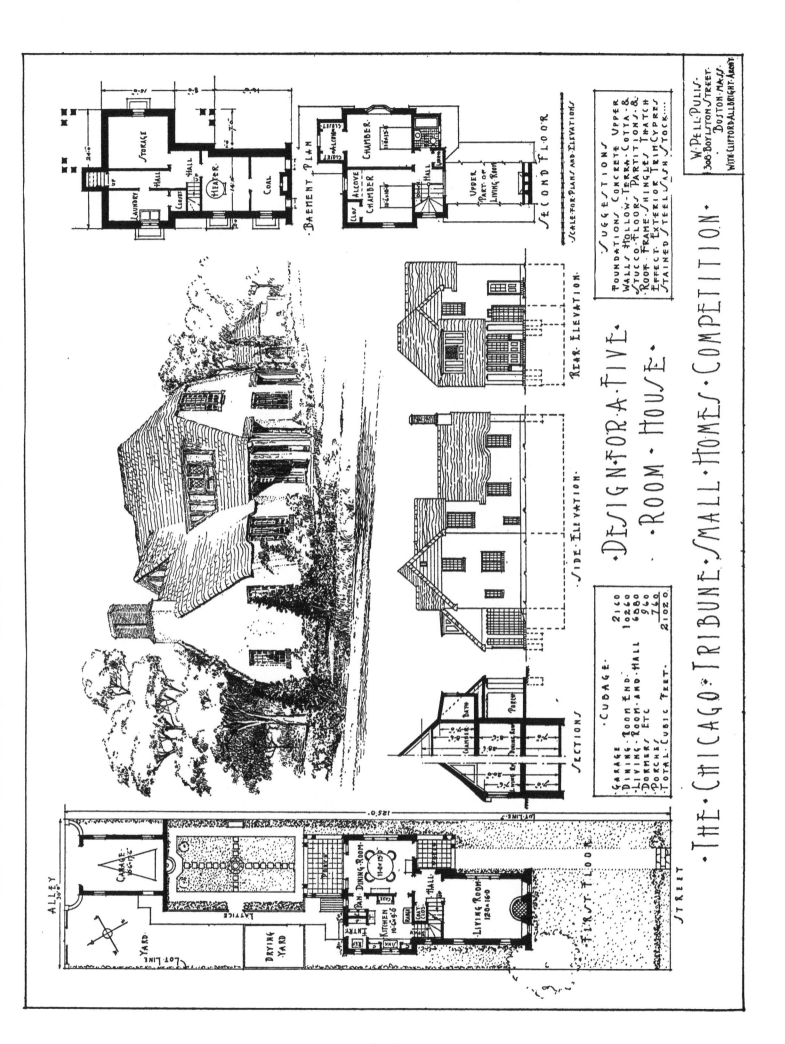

SECOND FLOOR

BAEMENT PLAN

SCALE FOR PLANS AND ELEVATIONS

SUGGESTIONS
FOUNDATIONS CONCRETE UPPER
WALLS HOLLOW TERRA COTTA &
STUCCO FLOORS PARTITIONS &
ROOF FRAME SHINGLE THATCH
EFFECT EXTERIOR TRIM CYPRES
STAINED STEEL SASH STOCK

W PELL PULIS
306 BOYLSTON STREET
BOSTON MASS
WITH CLIFFORD ALLBRIGHT ASSOC

REAR ELEVATION

SIDE ELEVATION

SECTIONS

CUBAGE
GARAGE   2160
DINING ROOM END   10260
LIVING ROOM AND HALL   6080
DORMERS ETC   960
PORCHES   760
TOTAL CUBIC FEET   21020

FIRST FLOOR

THE CHICAGO TRIBUNE SMALL HOMES COMPETITION

DESIGN FOR A FIVE ROOM HOUSE

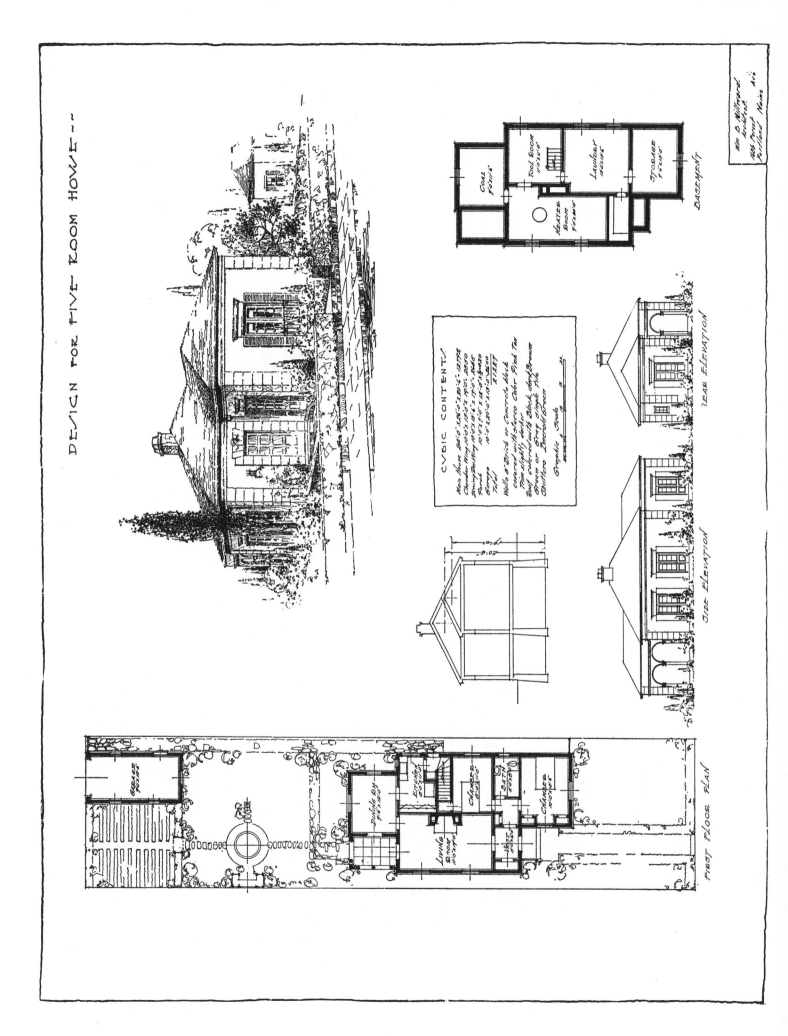

DESIGN FOR FIVE ROOM HOUSE

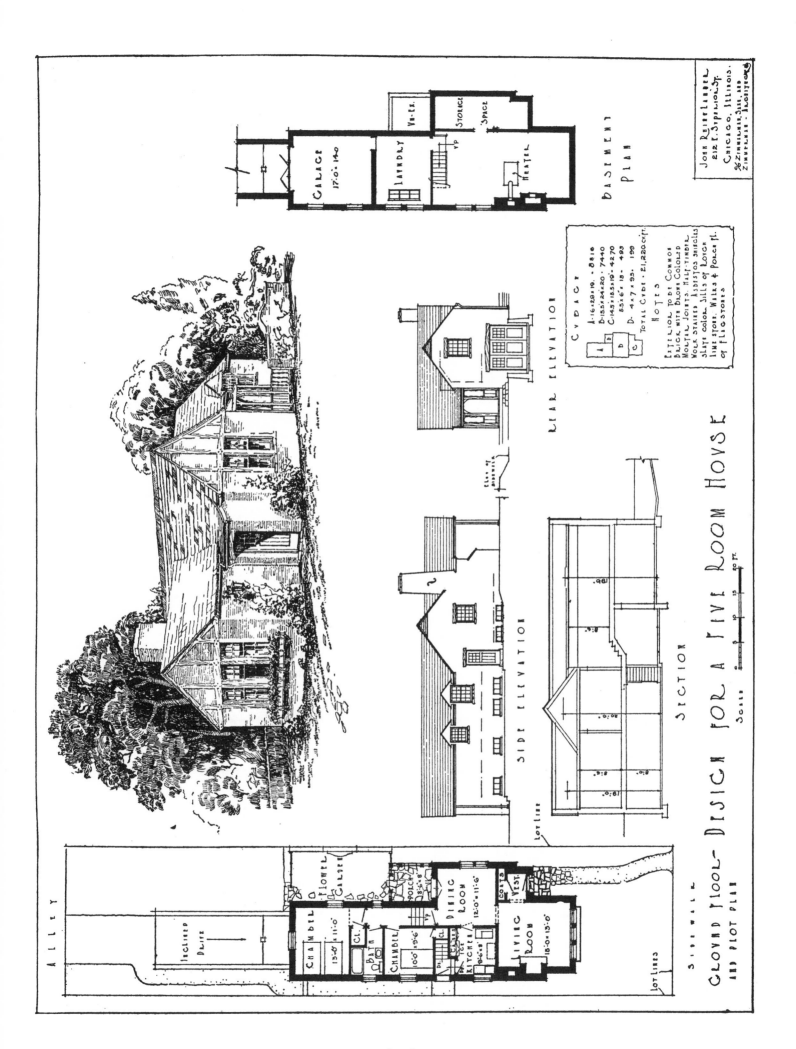

DESIGN FOR A FIVE ROOM HOUSE

DESIGN·FOR·A·
FIVE·ROOM·HOUSE·

PLAYGROUND

ALLEY

STREET

GARAGE
18'0"x34'0"

GARDEN

BED·ROOM
16'0"x12'0"

BED·ROOM
16'0"x12'0"

DINING·&·LIVING·ROOM
28'0"x15'0"

HALL

KITCHEN
10'0"x9'0"

·FIRST·FLOOR·&·PLOT·PLAN·

·SCALE·IN·FEET·

STORAGE

·ATTIC·&·ROOF·PLAN·

PLAY·&·GAME·RM·
16'6"x12'0"

LAUNDRY
17'0"x12'0"

BOILER·RM
13'0"x9'0"

FUEL·RM

VEGETABLE
ROOM
7'6"x9'0"

·BASEMENT·PLAN·

N

·REAR·ELEVATION·

·LONGITUDINAL·SECTION·

·SIDE·ELEVATION·

·CUBAGE·SCHEDULE·
UNDER·MAIN·ROOF·23'x34'x21'5" —— 11,668
REAR·BED·ROOM·17'x18'x10' —— 3,032
REMAINDER·OF·LINEAR·WALLS·x10' —— 3,790
BAY·WINDOW·10'x2'8"x8' —— 216
VEST·&·ICE·CHEST·5'0"x5'0"x18' —— 686
REAR·PORCH·5'x5'x9' —— 243
GARAGE·18'0"x34' —— 1,815
TOTAL·NO·CU·FT· —— 21,476

·BRIEF·DESCRIPTION·OF·MATERIALS·
THE·EXTERIOR·WALLS·MAY·BE·OF·CONCRETE·BLOCKS·INTERSPERSED·WITH·STONE·OR·BRICK·&·PARGED·OVER·WITH·
A·LIGHT·BUFF·STUCCO·SIMILAR·TO·AN·OLD·ENGLISH·COTTAGE.—·STEEL·CASEMENTS·SASH·&·SLATE·OR·SHINGLE·
ROOF·SHOULD·BE·USED·THROUGHOUT·—·HONEST·CONSTRUCTION·OF·WOOD·TRUSSES·&·PURLINS·FOR·ROOF·
OVER·LIVING·&·DINING·ROOM·WILL·LEND·ITSELF·AS·A·NICE·ARCHITECTURAL·FEATURE·FOR·THESE·
ROOMS·—·THE·REMAINDER·OF·THE·HOUSE·WILL·BE·SUCH·AS·TO·CONFORM·WITH·THE·PLANS·HERE·
AND·THE·REQUIREMENTS·OF·THE·SO·CALLED·"BUNGALOW"·SMALL·HOUSE·DWELLER·

·MR·CLYDE·E·LIGHT·
·DESIGNER·
3266·GENESEE·AVE·
DETROIT·MICH·

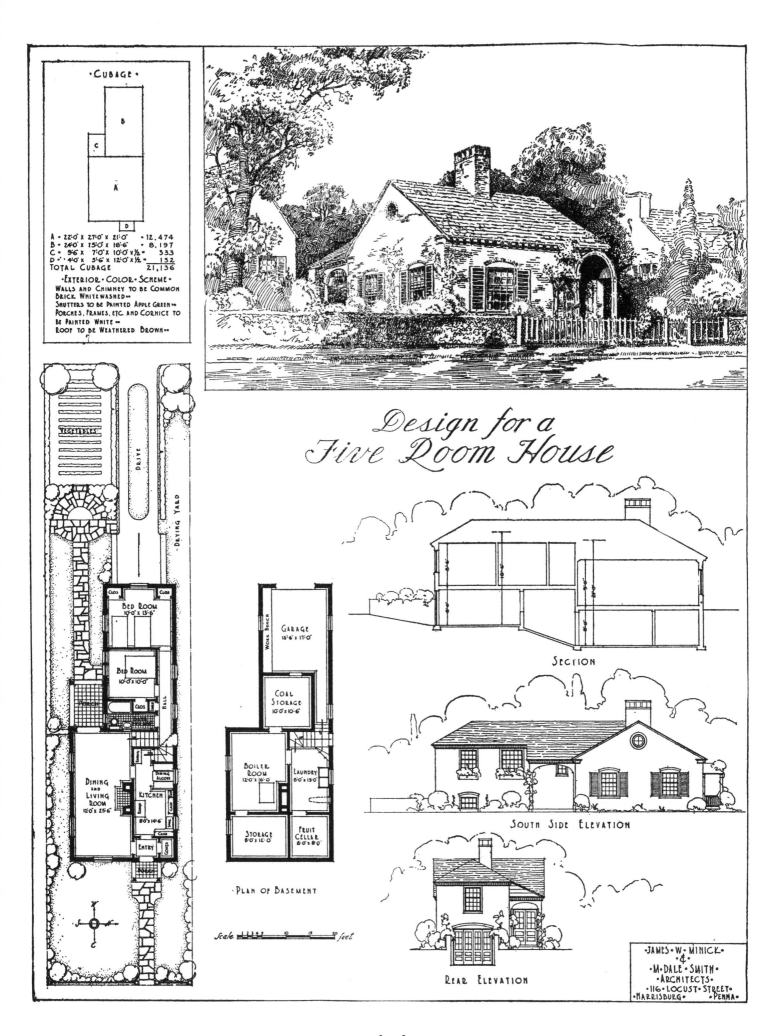

· CUBAGE ·

A · 22'-0" x 27'-0" x 21'-0" · 12,474
B · 24'-0" x 15'-0" x 18'-6" · 8,197
C · 9'-6" x 7'-0" x 10'-0" x ½ · 333
D · 4'-0" x 5'-6" x 12'-0" x ½ · 132
TOTAL CUBAGE   21,136

· EXTERIOR · COLOR · SCHEME ·
WALLS AND CHIMNEY TO BE COMMON
BRICK WHITEWASHED ··
SHUTTERS TO BE PAINTED APPLE GREEN ··
PORCHES, FRAMES, ETC. AND CORNICE TO
BE PAINTED WHITE ··
ROOF TO BE WEATHERED BROWN ··

VEGETABLES

DRIVE

DRYING YARD

BED ROOM
10'-0" x 13'-6"

CLOS.   CLOS.

BED ROOM
10'-0" x 10'-0"

CLOS.

HALL

Porch

DINING
AND
LIVING
ROOM
12'-0" x 25'-6"

KITCHEN
8'-0" x 14'-6"

DINING ALCOVE

ENTRY

WORK BENCH

GARAGE
13'-6" x 17'-0"

COAL
STORAGE
10'-0" x 10'-6"

BOILER
ROOM
12'-0" x 16'-0"

LAUNDRY
6'-0" x 13'-0"

STORAGE
8'-0" x 12'-0"

FRUIT
CELLAR
6'-0" x 8'-0"

PLAN OF BASEMENT

Scale 5 10 15 20 feet

Design for a
Five Room House

SECTION

SOUTH SIDE ELEVATION

REAR ELEVATION

· JAMES · W · MINICK ·
· & ·
· M · DALE · SMITH ·
· ARCHITECTS ·
· 116 · LOCUST · STREET ·
· HARRISBURG ·   · PENNA ·

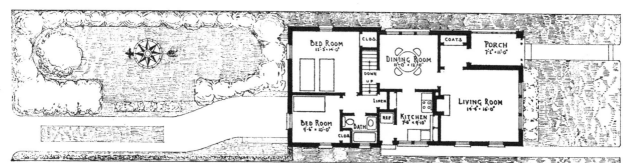

FIRST FLOOR PLAN

Bed Room
11'-3"×14'-0"

CLOS.

DINING ROOM
11'-0"×12'-0"

COATS

PORCH
7'-2"×11'-0"

DOWN

UP

LINEN

LIVING ROOM
19'-4"×16'-0"

Bed Room
9'-6"×10'-0"

BATH

REF.

KITCHEN
7'-0"×9'-10"

CLOS.

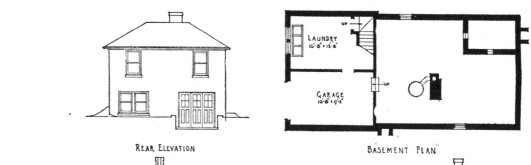

REAR ELEVATION

BASEMENT PLAN

LAUNDRY
10'-6"×13'-8"

UP

GARAGE
10'-6"×17'-2"

UP

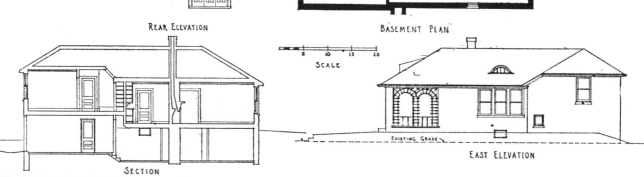

SECTION

SCALE
5   10   15   20

EAST ELEVATION

EXISTING GRADE

CUBIC CONTENTS
REAR 24'×19'×19' = 8664
FRONT 25'×29'×19¼' = 12455
Cu. Ft. 21,119

DESIGN FOR A FIVE ROOM HOUSE

PAUL F. MANN
37 ALLEN ST.
BUFFALO N.Y.

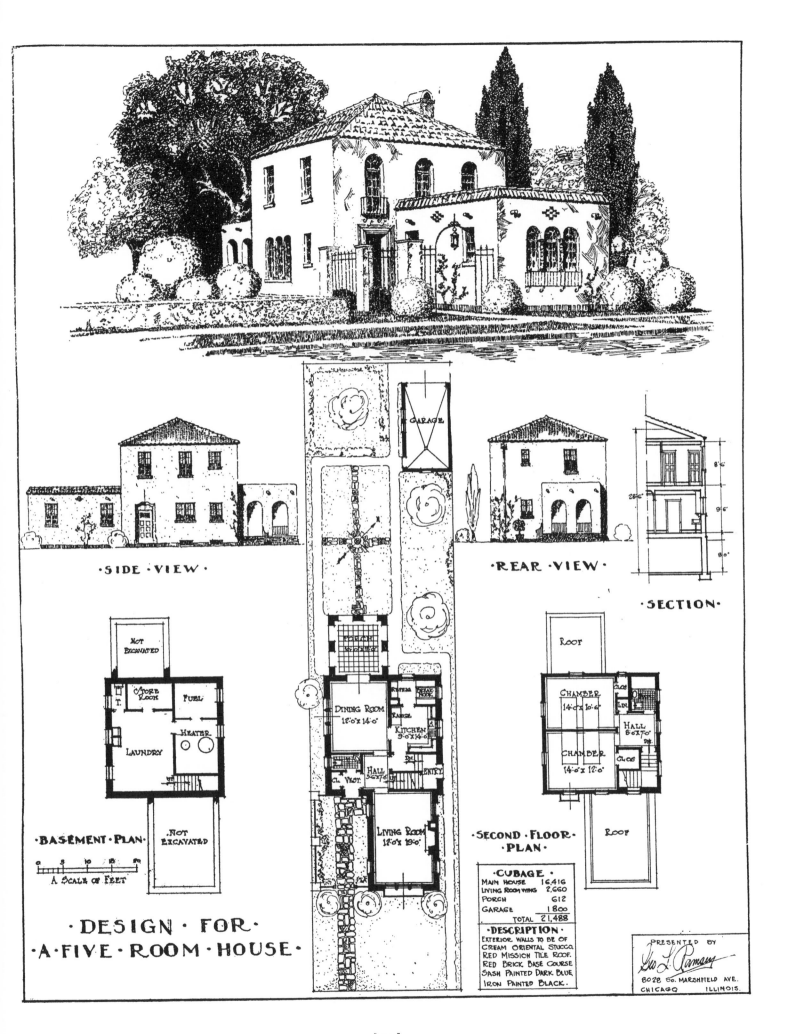

· SIDE · VIEW ·

· REAR · VIEW ·

· SECTION ·

· BASEMENT · PLAN ·

A SCALE OF FEET

NOT EXCAVATED

STORE ROOM

FUEL

HEATER

LAUNDRY

NOT EXCAVATED

GARAGE

PORCH

DINING ROOM
18'-0" x 14'-0"

KITCHEN
9'-0" x 14'-0"

RANGE

HALL
3'-6" x 7'-6"

CL. VEST.

ENTRY

LIVING ROOM
18'-0" x 19'-0"

· SECOND · FLOOR ·
· PLAN ·

ROOF

CHAMBER
14'-0" x 10'-6"

CHAMBER
14'-0" x 12'-0"

HALL
8'-0" x 7'-0"

ROOF

· DESIGN · FOR ·
· A · FIVE · ROOM · HOUSE ·

· CUBAGE ·
MAIN HOUSE   16,416
LIVING ROOM WING   2,660
PORCH   612
GARAGE   1,800
TOTAL   21,488

· DESCRIPTION ·
EXTERIOR WALLS TO BE OF
CREAM ORIENTAL STUCCO.
RED MISSION TILE ROOF.
RED BRICK BASE COURSE.
SASH PAINTED DARK BLUE
IRON PAINTED BLACK.

PRESENTED BY
Geo. L. Ramsey
8028 So. MARSHFIELD AVE.
CHICAGO   ILLINOIS.

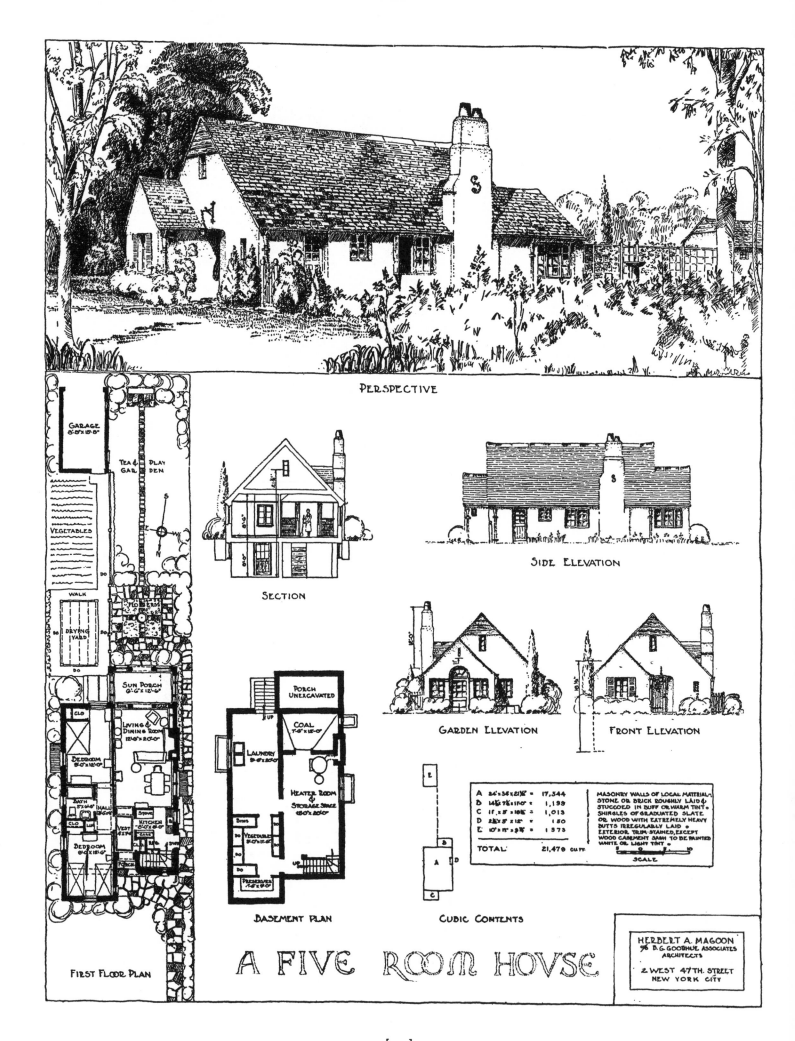

PERSPECTIVE

SECTION

SIDE ELEVATION

GARDEN ELEVATION

FRONT ELEVATION

FIRST FLOOR PLAN

BASEMENT PLAN

CUBIC CONTENTS

A	24'×36'×21½'	=	17,544
B	14½'×7½'×11'0"	=	1,198
C	17'×8'×10½'	=	1,013
D	2½'×5'×12'	=	150
E	10'×17'×8¾'	=	1,573
TOTAL:			21,478 CU.FT.

MASONRY WALLS OF LOCAL MATERIAL — STONE OR BRICK ROUGHLY LAID & STUCCOED IN BUFF OR WARM TINT • SHINGLES OF GRADUATED SLATE OR WOOD WITH EXTREMELY HEAVY BUTTS IRREGULARLY LAID • EXTERIOR TRIM STAINED, EXCEPT WOOD CASEMENT SASH TO BE PAINTED WHITE OR LIGHT TINT •

SCALE

A FIVE ROOM HOUSE

HERBERT A. MAGOON
℅ B.G. GOODHUE ASSOCIATES
ARCHITECTS

2 WEST 47TH STREET
NEW YORK CITY

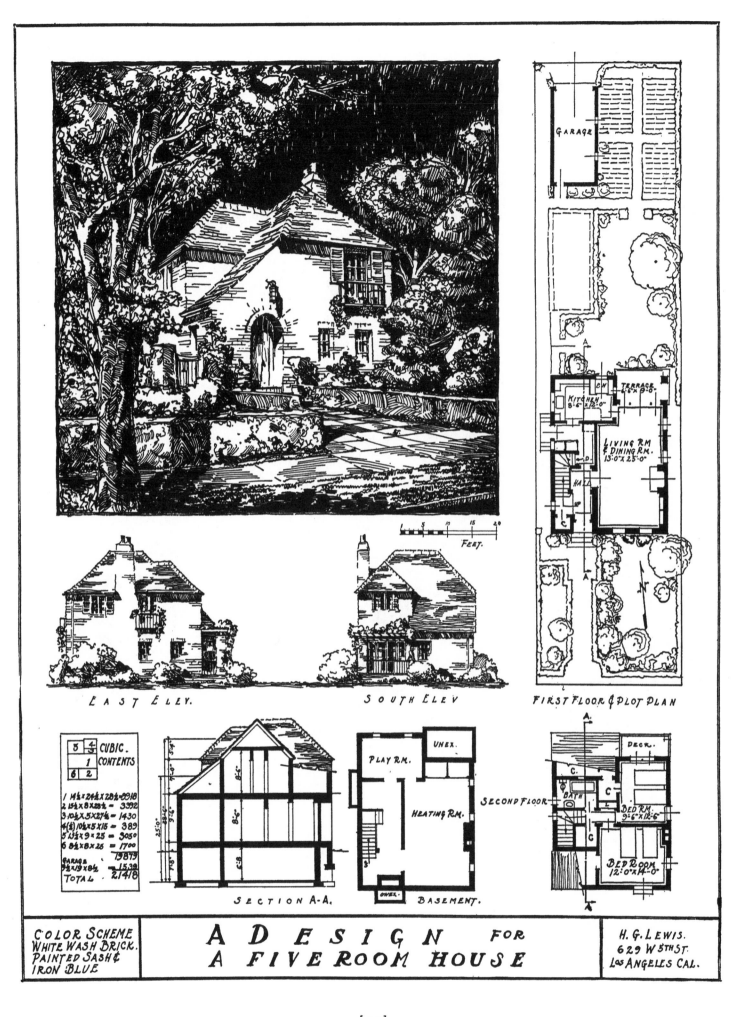

GARAGE

KITCHEN
8'-6" X 12'-0"

TERRACE
8'-6" X 9'-0"

LIVING RM.
& DINING RM.
13'-0" X 25'-0"

HALL

FIRST FLOOR & PLOT PLAN

EAST ELEV.

SOUTH ELEV

FEET.

5   4   CUBIC.
    1   CONTENTS
6   2

1 14½ x 24½ x 28½ = 2918
2 151 x 8 x 28½ = 3392
3 10½ x 5 x 27½ = 1430
4(½) 10½ x 5 x 15 = 389
5 6½ x 9 x 25 = 3050
6 8½ x 8 x 25 = 1700
                19879
GARAGE
9½ x 19 x 8½   1539
TOTAL   21418

SECTION A-A.

PLAY RM.

UNEX.

HEATING RM.

UNEX.

BASEMENT.

DECK.

BATH

BED RM
9'-6" X 12'-6"

SECOND FLOOR

BED ROOM
12'-0" X 14'-0"

COLOR SCHEME
WHITE WASH BRICK.
PAINTED SASH &
IRON BLUE

A DESIGN FOR
A FIVE ROOM HOUSE

H. G. LEWIS.
629 W 5TH ST.
LOS ANGELES CAL.

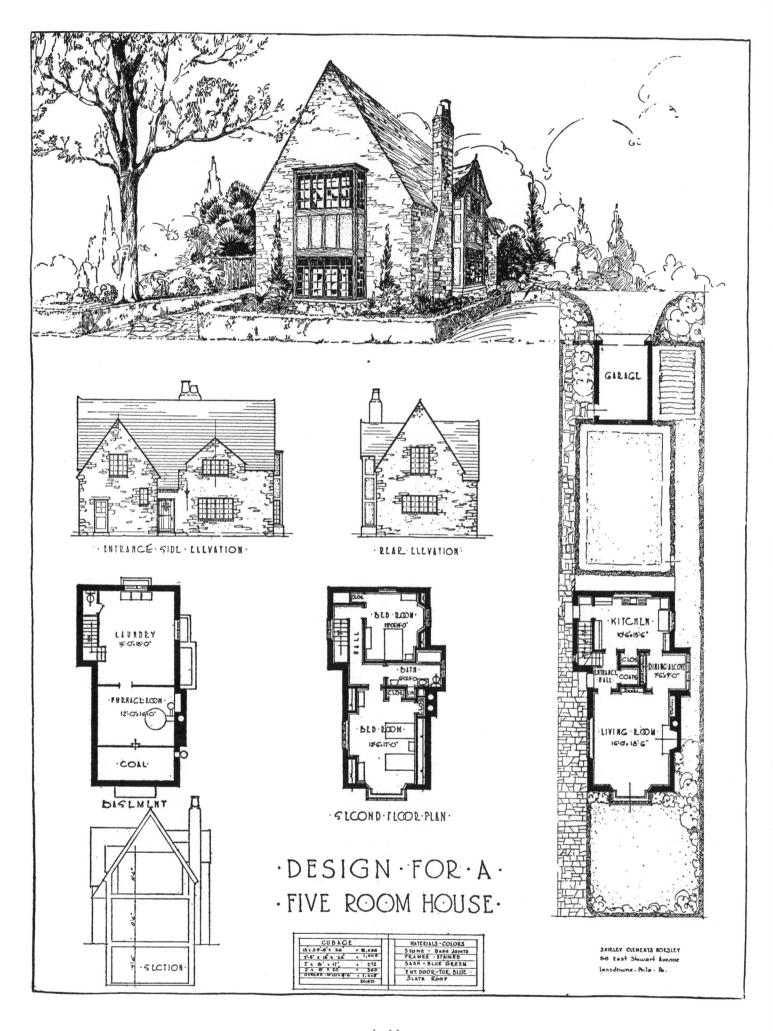

· ENTRANCE · SIDE · ELEVATION ·

· REAR · ELEVATION ·

GARAGE

LAUNDRY
15'·0"·18'·0"

FURNACE·ROOM
12'·0"·16'·0"

·COAL·

·BASEMENT·

CLOS.

BED·ROOM
12'·0"·14'·0"

HALL

BATH
6'·6"·10'·0"

CLOS. LIN

BED·ROOM
12'·6"·17'·0"

·SECOND·FLOOR·PLAN·

KITCHEN
10'·6"·13'·6"

CLOS

ENTRANCE
HALL   CLOS
       COATS

DINING·ALCOVE
7'·6"·9'·0"

LIVING·ROOM
15'·0"·18'·6"

·SECTION·

· DESIGN · FOR · A ·
FIVE ROOM HOUSE·

CUBAGE		
13'·39'·6"·26"	"	18,486
2'·8"·16'·26"	"	1,005
2'·8"·17"	"	272
2'·8'·20	"	360
8'·8'·10·11'·8"·6'	"	1,448
		24,571

MATERIALS·COLORS
STONE - DASH JOINTS
FRAMES - STAINED
SASH - BLUE GREEN
·ENT·DOOR-TUR·BLUE·
SLATE ROOF

SHIRLEY CLEMENTS HORSLEY
56 East Stewart Avenue
Lansdowne - Phila - Pa.

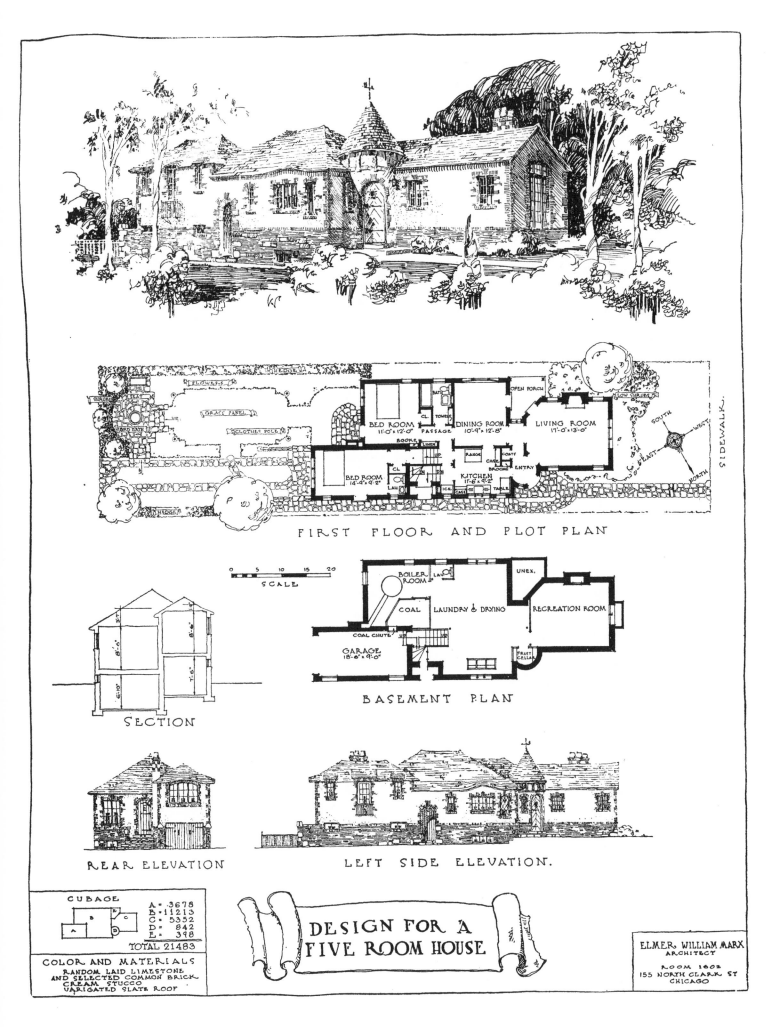

FIRST FLOOR AND PLOT PLAN

BASEMENT PLAN

SECTION

REAR ELEVATION

LEFT SIDE ELEVATION.

CUBAGE

A = 3678
B = 11213
C = 5352
D = 842
E = 398

TOTAL 21483

COLOR AND MATERIALS
RANDOM LAID LIMESTONE
AND SELECTED COMMON BRICK
CREAM STUCCO
VARIGATED SLATE ROOF

DESIGN FOR A
FIVE ROOM HOUSE

ELMER WILLIAM MARX
ARCHITECT

ROOM 1602
155 NORTH CLARK ST
CHICAGO

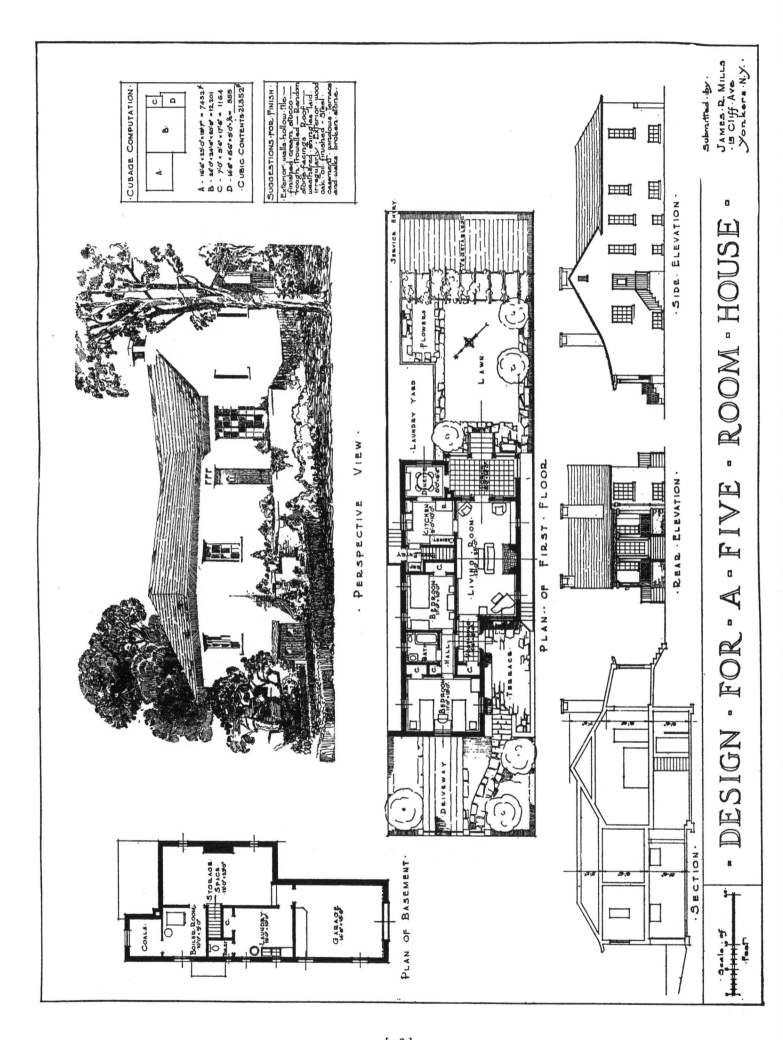

· CUBAGE · COMPUTATION ·

A · 146'·125'·0'·187' = 7452 f
B · 240'·245'·259' = 12,201
C · 70'·58'·178' = 1164
D · 146'·86'·90'% = 555
· CUBIC · CONTENTS · 21,352 ᶠ

· SUGGESTIONS · FOR · FINISH ·

Exterior walls hollow tile—
finished cream stucco
rough trowelled — Random
stone facings Roof
weathered shingles laid
irregular. Exterior wood
oak oil finished · Steel
casement windows. Terrace
and walks broken stone.

· PERSPECTIVE · VIEW ·

· PLAN · OF · BASEMENT ·

· PLAN · OF · FIRST · FLOOR ·

· SIDE · ELEVATION ·

· REAR · ELEVATION ·

· SECTION ·

· DESIGN · FOR · A · FIVE · ROOM · HOUSE ·

Submitted by
James R. Mills
15 Cliff Ave
Yonkers N.Y.

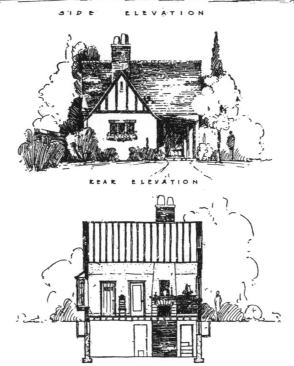

SIDE ELEVATION

REAR ELEVATION

SECTION

· C U B A G E ·

FRONT WING 14½ x 20¼ x 30 = 8874
REAR WING 14½ x 20¼ x 13 = 3620
CENTER WING 14½ x 21¼ x 24 = 7398
BACK PORCH 7 x 5½ x 8 = 308
FRONT PORCH 5 x 3½ x 8 = 140
GARAGE 9 x 8½ x 13 = 994
TOTAL 21,334

BUILDING NOTES
HOUSE TO BE BRICK COVERED
WITH FAINT CREAM STUCCO
HALF TIMBER STAINED BROWN
ROOF OF ENGLISH TILE OR SLATE
VARIGATED BRICK FOR CHIMNEY
HEWN OAK ENTRY DOOR

SERVICE

GARAGE
9'-0" x 13'-0"

KITCHEN
9'-6" x 13'-0"

LIVING & DINING
13'-0" x 22'-6"

BED ROOM
9'-0" x 10'-0"

CLOS

BATH
5'-0" x 9'-0"

CLOSET

BED ROOM
10'-0" x 13'-0"

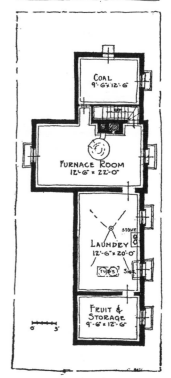

COAL
9'-6" x 12'-6"

FURNACE ROOM
12'-6" x 22'-0"

LAUNDRY
12'-6" x 20'-0"

FRUIT & STORAGE
9'-6" x 12'-6"

N

Design For A Five Room House

WILLIAM A. ROLLESTON
255 W 97TH STREET
NEW YORK CITY
NEW YORK.

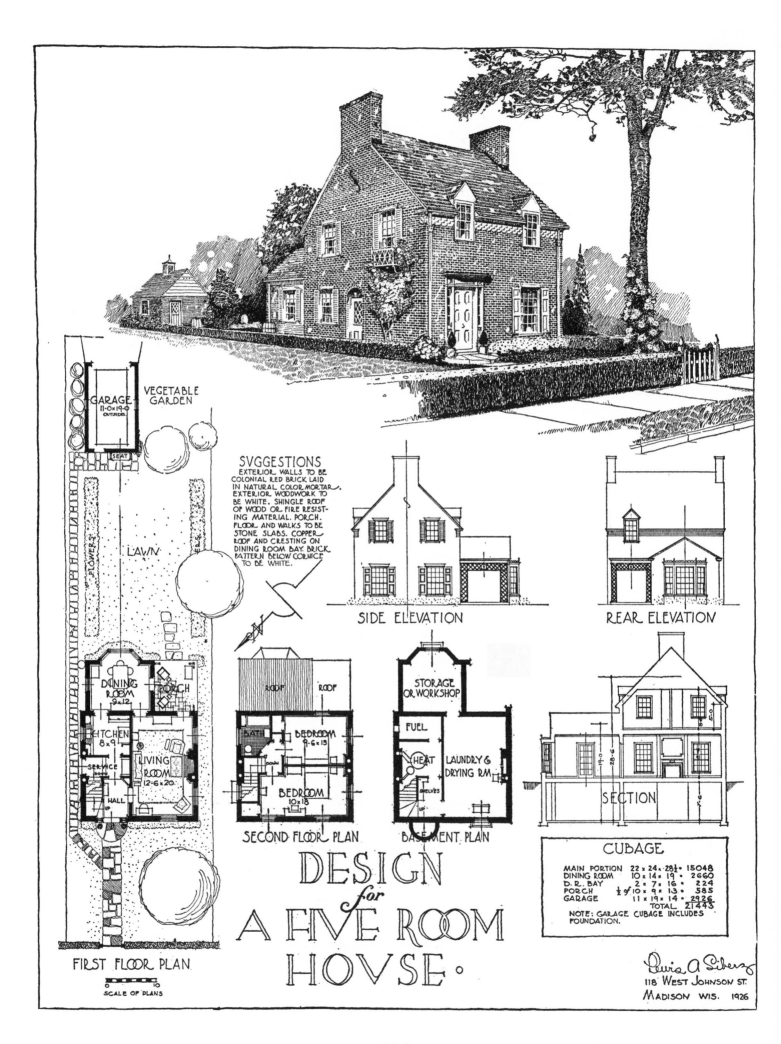

GARAGE
11-0x19-0
OUTSIDE

VEGETABLE
GARDEN

SEAT

LAWN

FLOWERS

FIRST FLOOR PLAN

0 __ 10
SCALE OF PLANS

DINING
ROOM
9×12

PORCH

KITCHEN
8×9

SERVICE
DOWN

LIVING
ROOM
12·6×20

HALL
UP

SVGGESTIONS

EXTERIOR WALLS TO BE
COLONIAL RED BRICK LAID
IN NATURAL COLOR MORTAR.
EXTERIOR WOODWORK TO
BE WHITE. SHINGLE ROOF
OF WOOD OR FIRE RESIST-
ING MATERIAL. PORCH.
FLOOR AND WALKS TO BE
STONE SLABS. COPPER
ROOF AND CRESTING ON
DINING ROOM BAY. BRICK
PATTERN BELOW CORNICE
TO BE WHITE.

SIDE ELEVATION

REAR ELEVATION

ROOF   ROOF

BATH

BEDROOM
9-6×13

DOWN

BEDROOM
10×18

SECOND FLOOR PLAN

STORAGE
OR WORKSHOP

FUEL

HEAT

LAUNDRY &
DRYING RM

SHELVES

UP

BASEMENT PLAN

SECTION

28-6   19-0   5-0   7-6

DESIGN
for
A FIVE ROOM
HOVSE

CUBAGE

MAIN PORTION	22 × 24 × 28½ =	15048
DINING ROOM	10 × 14 × 19 =	2660
D. R. BAY	2 × 7 × 16 =	224
PORCH	½ of 10 × 9 × 13 =	585
GARAGE	11 × 19 × 14 =	2926
	TOTAL	21443

NOTE: GARAGE CUBAGE INCLUDES
FOUNDATION.

Leura A Liberg
118 WEST JOHNSON ST.
MADISON WIS. 1926

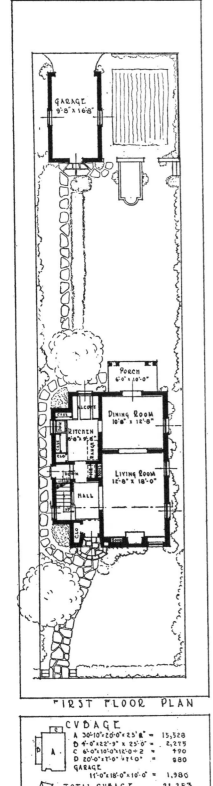

GARAGE
9'-8" x 16'-8"

Porch
6'-0" x 10'-0"

Dining Room
10'-8" x 12'-8"

KITCHEN
8'-8"

Living Room
12'-8" x 18'-0"

HALL

FIRST FLOOR PLAN

CUBAGE
A 30'-10" x 20'-0" x 25'-8" = 15,528
B 4'-0" x 22'-9" x 25'-0" =   2,275
C 6'-0" x 10'-0" x 12'-0" ÷ 2 =   490
D 20'-0" x 7'-0" x 7'-0" =   980
GARAGE
    11'-0" x 18'-0" x 10'-0" =   1,980
TOTAL CUBAGE 21,253
CONSTRUCTION TO BE COMMON
BRICK VENEER, WALLS TO BE PAINTED
WHITE, ROOF PEA GREEN SHINGLES

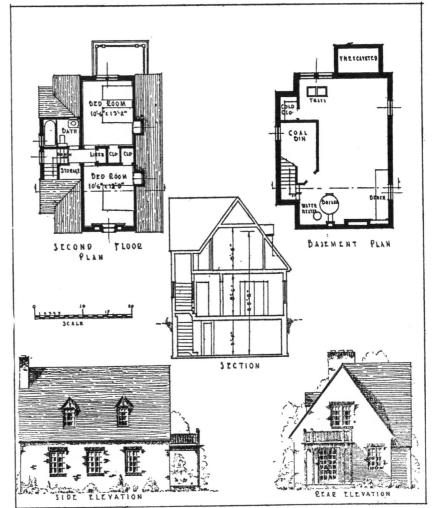

BED ROOM
10'-6" x 13'-2"

BATH

BED ROOM
10'-6" x 12'-0"

LINEN CLO CLO

STORAGE

SECOND FLOOR PLAN

SCALE

SECTION

SIDE ELEVATION

UNEXCAVATED

TRAPS

COLD CLO

COAL BIN

WATER HEATER

BASEMENT PLAN

REAR ELEVATION

DESIGN FOR A FIVE ROOM HOUSE

SUBMITTED BY
ONNIE MANRRI
3801 GLENWOOD RD
CLEVELAND HEIGHTS
OHIO

DESIGN FOR A FIVE ROOM HOUSE

WEST ELEVATION

REAR ELEVATION

SECTION

BASEMENT PLAN.

SECOND FLOOR PLAN.

FIRST FLOOR AND PLOT PLAN.

CHARLES A. MARKLEY.
255 GENESEE ST.
UTICA. N.Y.

CUBICAL CONTENTS
LIVING ROOM WING - 7167
DINING ROOM WING - 10176
GARAGE - 2550
PORCH - 1118
TOTAL 21127 CU.FT.

GRAPHIC SCALE

COLORS & MATERIAL:
ROOF - VARIEGATED SLATE.
WALLS - GREY STONE VENEER.
EXT. WOOD - STAINED BROWN.
BRICK - RED BROWN.
FLAGSTONE PORCH FLOOR.

GARAGE
KITCHEN
DINING RM.
LIVING ROOM
ENTRY

HEATER RM.
COAL
LAUNDRY

BED ROOM
HALL
BATH
BED ROOM
CLOS.

[62]

DESIGN FOR
A FIVE
ROOM HOUSE

MATERIALS

Exterior finish to be
Chicago common brick with
Wisconsin field stone and
Stucco in slightly wavy
Uneven surfaces.
Door and window Trim and
Timber work to be rough
Sawn Oak stained weathered
Brown. Wood shingle
Roof in wavy lines.
Tone deep weathered
Brown at eaves To a
Lighter brown at ridges.

CUBAGE

A	19'-6"x36'-6"x20'-9"=	14,825
B	15'-7"x45'-0"x4'-5"=	1,377
C	12'-4"x4'-0"x16'-6"=	827
D	6'-6"x9'-6"x12'-2"=	371
E	13'-0"x10'-6"x19'-2"=	2,574
Dormer		128
Garage		1,411
TOTAL		21,493

WILLARD C. WALKER
ARCHITECT
58 EAST WASHINGTON STREET
CHICAGO

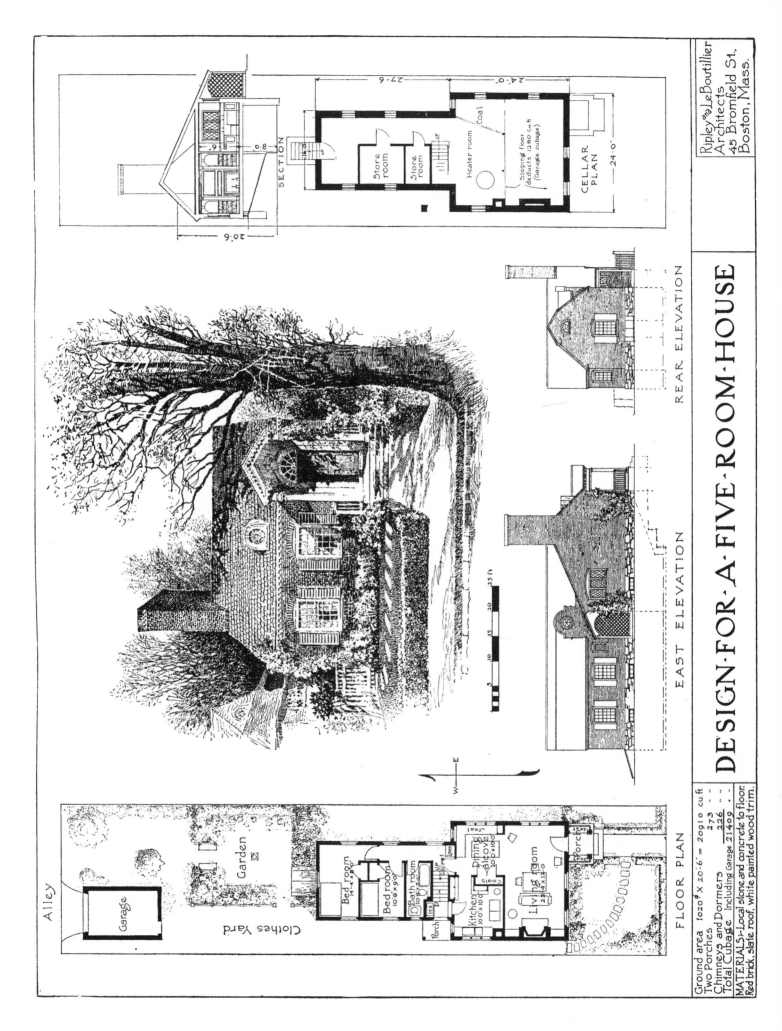

SECTION

CELLAR PLAN

24'-0"

27'-6"

Store room

Store room

Heater room

Coal

Sloping floor (deducts 1280 cu.ft. (garage cubage)

24'-0"

20'-6"

9'-8"

8'-0"

REAR ELEVATION

EAST ELEVATION

5 10 15 20 25 ft

W   E

FLOOR PLAN

Alley

Garage

Garden

Clothes Yard

Bed room 14'-4" x 8'-0"

Bed room 10'-8" x 9'-0"

Bath room 10'-8" x 7'-2"

Kitchen 10'-0" x 10'-0"

Dining alcove 10'-0" x 10'-0"

Living room 22'-4" x 12'-0"

Porch

Porch

Ripley and LeBoutillier
Architects
45 Bromfield St.
Boston, Mass.

DESIGN·FOR·A·FIVE·ROOM·HOUSE

Ground area 1020# x 20'-6" = 20910 cu.ft.
Two Porches   273   "   "
Chimneys and Dormers 226   "   "
Total Cubage Including Garage 21409 "   "
MATERIALS:—Local stone and concrete to floor.
Red brick, slate roof, white painted wood trim.

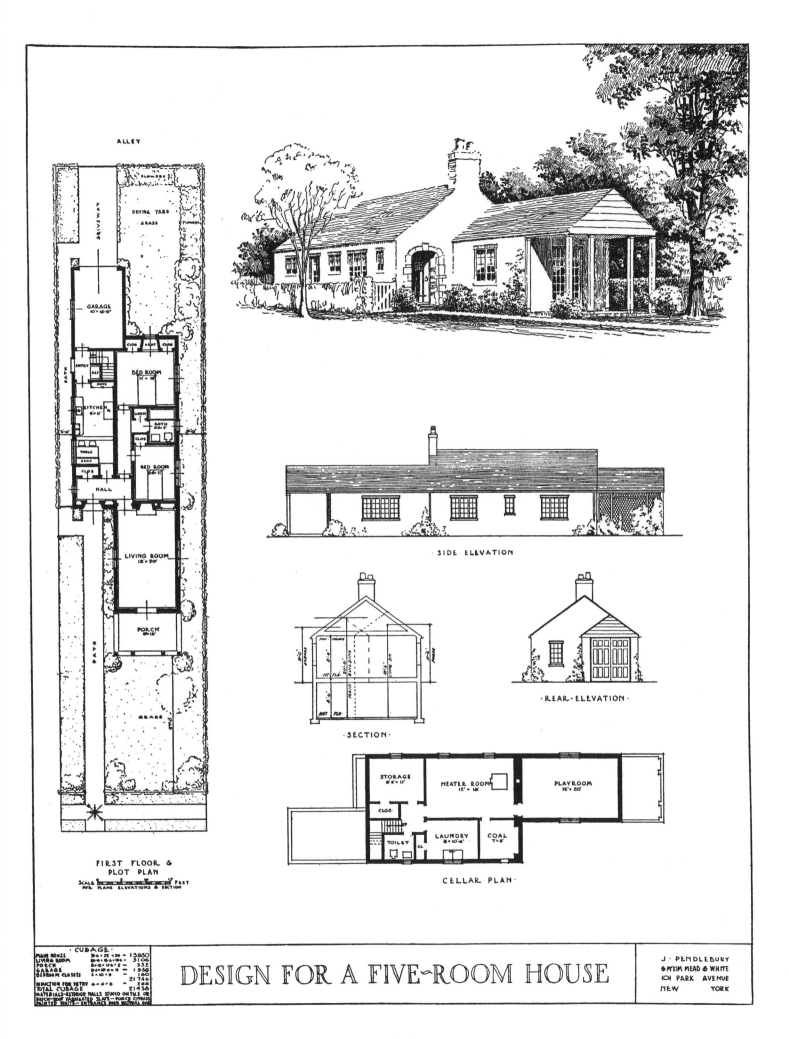

ALLEY

DRYING YARD
GRASS

GARAGE
10' x 18'-0"

DRIVEWAY

PATH

ENTRY

CLOS · SEAT · CLOS

BED ROOM
11' x 11'

KITCHEN
8' x 11'

LINEN

BATH
5'-6" x 7'

TABLE
SEAT

CLOS

CLOS

BED ROOM
9'-6" x 11'

HALL

LIVING ROOM
12' x 20'

PORCH
6' x 18'

PATH

GRASS

FIRST FLOOR &
PLOT PLAN

Scale
FOR PLANS ELEVATIONS & SECTION

· SIDE · ELEVATION ·

· SECTION ·

· REAR · ELEVATION ·

STORAGE
8'-6" x 11'

HEATER ROOM
12' x 18'

PLAYROOM
12' x 20'

CLOS

TOILET

LAUNDRY
8' x 10'-6"

COAL
7' x 8'

· CELLAR PLAN ·

· CUBAGE ·
MAIN HOUSE   54 x 75 x 70 = 13950
LIVING ROOM   34 x 18 x 10½ = 3106
PORCH   8½ x 18½ x 2 = 332
GARAGE   9 x 18½ x 11½ = 1958
BED ROOM CLOSETS 3 x 10 x 9 = 180
                              21746
REDUCTION FOR ENTRY 6 x 6 x 8 = 288
TOTAL CUBAGE   21458
MATERIALS—EXTERIOR WALLS STUCCO ON TILE OR
BRICK—ROOF VARIEGATED SLATE—PORCH CYPRESS
PAINTED WHITE—ENTRANCE DOOR NATURAL OAK

DESIGN FOR A FIVE-ROOM HOUSE

J · PENDLEBURY
McKIM MEAD & WHITE
101 PARK AVENUE
NEW YORK

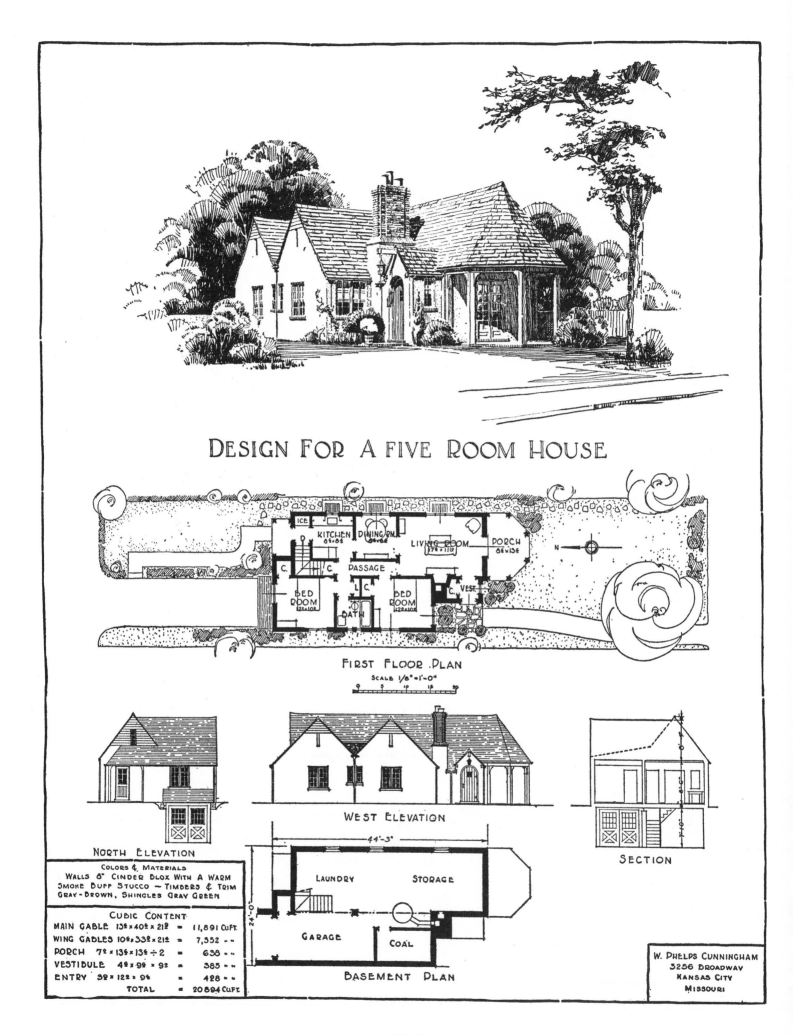

DESIGN FOR A FIVE ROOM HOUSE

FIRST FLOOR PLAN

SCALE 1/8"=1'-0"

ICE | KITCHEN 8'×8' | DINING RM 8'×8' | LIVING ROOM 17'6"×11'6" | PORCH 8'×13'6"

C. | C. | PASSAGE | N | VEST.

BED ROOM 12'×10' | L.C. | BED ROOM 12'8"×10'

BATH

NORTH ELEVATION

WEST ELEVATION

SECTION

COLORS & MATERIALS
WALLS 8" CINDER BLOX WITH A WARM
SMOKE BUFF STUCCO — TIMBERS & TRIM
GRAY-BROWN, SHINGLES GRAY GREEN

CUBIC CONTENT

MAIN GABLE 13'×40'×21'	=	11,891 CU.FT.
WING GABLES 10'×33'×21'	=	7,552 "
PORCH 7'×13'×13'÷2	=	638 "
VESTIBULE 4'×9'×9'	=	385 "
ENTRY 5'×12'×9'	=	428 "
TOTAL	=	20,894 CU.FT.

BASEMENT PLAN

44'-3"

24'-0"

LAUNDRY | STORAGE

GARAGE | COAL

W. PHELPS CUNNINGHAM
3256 BROADWAY
KANSAS CITY
MISSOURI

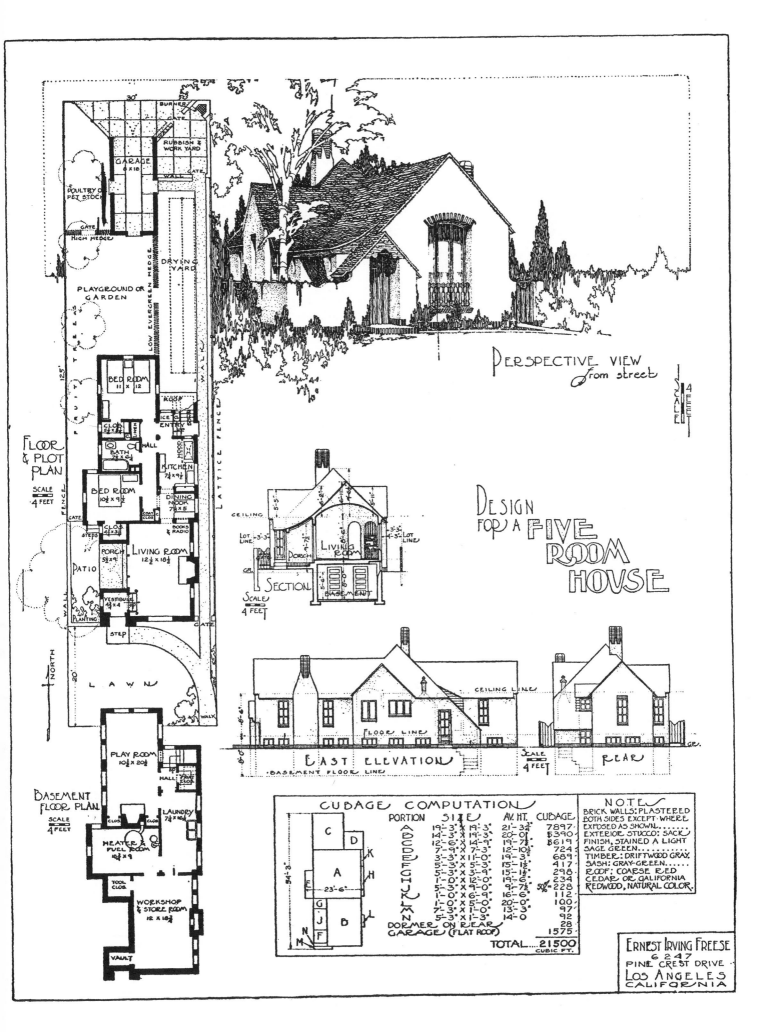

FLOOR & PLOT PLAN
SCALE 4 FEET

GARAGE 6 x 18
BURNER GATE
RUBBISH & WORK YARD
POULTRY OR PET STOCK
GATE HIGH HEDGE
PLAYGROUND OR GARDEN
DRYING YARD
LOW EVERGREEN HEDGE
FRUIT TREES
125'
30'

BED ROOM 11 x 12
ROOM
CLOS
ICE
ENTRY
LINEN
HALL
BATH 7½ x 6½
KITCHEN 7½ x 9½
BED ROOM 10½ x 9½
DINING NOOK 7½ x 5
CLOS
COAT CLOS
BOOKS RADIO
STEPS
PORCH 5½ x 9
LIVING ROOM 12½ x 18½
GATE
PATIO
VESTIBULE 4½ x 4
PLANTING
STEP
GATE
LATTICE FENCE
WALK
FENCE WALL
20'
NORTH
LAWN
WALK

PERSPECTIVE VIEW from street
SCALE 4 FEET

CEILING
LOT LINE 3'-3"
5'-5"
PORCH
LIVING ROOM
LOT LINE 3'-3"
BASEMENT
SECTION
SCALE 4 FEET

DESIGN FOR A FIVE ROOM HOUSE

CEILING LINE
FLOOR LINE
EAST ELEVATION
BASEMENT FLOOR LINE
SCALE 4 FEET
REAR

BASEMENT FLOOR PLAN
SCALE 4 FEET

PLAY ROOM 10½ x 20½
HALL
FRUIT CLOS
CLOS
CLOS
LAUNDRY 7½ x 16½
HEATER & FUEL ROOM 10½ x 9
TOOL CLOS
WORKSHOP & STORE ROOM 12 x 18½
VAULT

CUBAGE COMPUTATION

PORTION	SIZE	AV. HT.	CUBAGE
A	19'-3" x 19'-3"	21'-3¾"	7897
B	14'-3" x 19'-3"	20'-0½"	5390
C	12'-6" x 14'-9"	19'-7"	3619
D	7'-9" x 7'-3"	12'-10½"	724
E	3'-3" x 11'-0"	19'-3"	689
F	5'-3" x 5'-3"	15'-1½"	417
G	5'-3" x 3'-9"	15'-1"	298
H	1'-0" x 12'-0"	19'-6"	234
I	5'-3" x 9'-0"	9'-7½" 50%	228
J	5'-3" x 6'-9"	16'-6"	112
K	1'-0" x 5'-0"	20'-0"	100
L	1'-0" x 5'-0"	13'-3"	97
M	5'-3" x 1'-0"	14'-0"	92
N	5'-3" x 1'-3"		28
DORMER ON REAR			
GARAGE (FLAT ROOF)			1575

54'-3"
23'-6"

TOTAL....21500 CUBIC FT.

NOTE:
BRICK WALLS: PLASTERED BOTH SIDES EXCEPT WHERE EXPOSED AS SHOWN. EXTERIOR STUCCO: SACK FINISH, STAINED A LIGHT SAGE GREEN. TIMBER: DRIFTWOOD GRAY. SASH: GRAY-GREEN. ROOF: COARSE RED CEDAR OR CALIFORNIA REDWOOD, NATURAL COLOR.

ERNEST IRVING FREESE
6247 PINE CREST DRIVE
LOS ANGELES CALIFORNIA

Design
for

A FIVE ROOM HOUSE

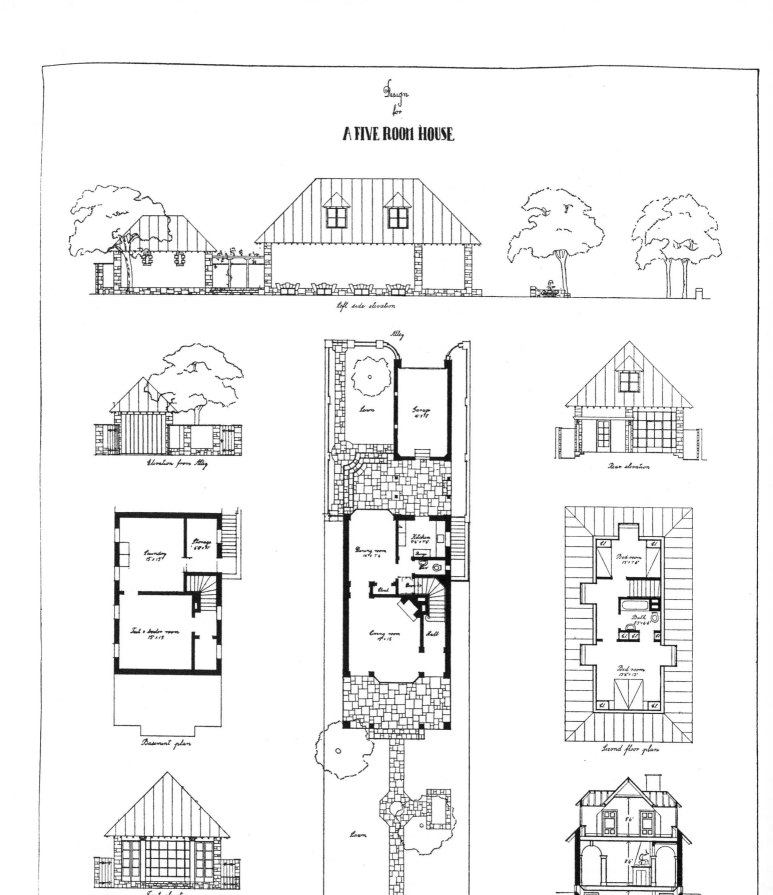

Left side elevation

Elevation from Alley

Rear elevation

Basement plan

First floor plan

Second floor plan

Front elevation

Section

Carl Jensen
Box 1242
Sarasota Florida

The house is to be build of darkred bricks with darkgray Pilasters. The roof is to be thatched with roofing in two colours. The porch may be screened or enclosed in glass. The flagstones on the front and back yard are made of sandstone in a light colour. The house contents 18755 cubic feet the Garage 2760 cb ft.

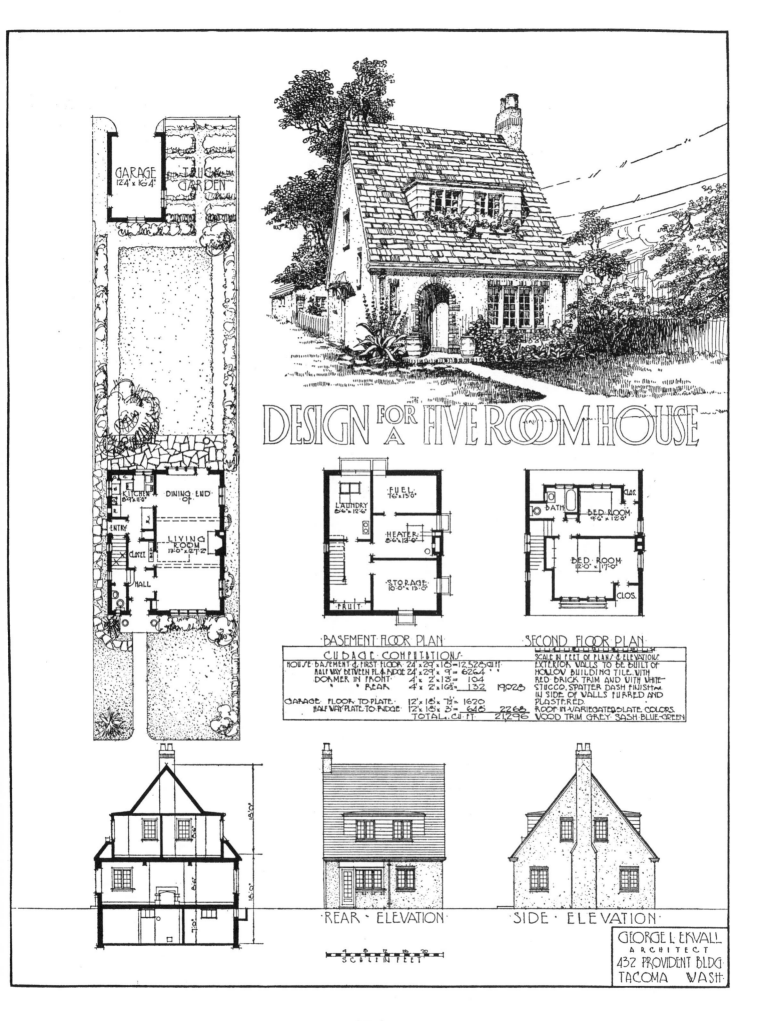

GARAGE
12'4" x 16'4"

TRUCK GARDEN

KITCHEN
8'9" x 11'0"

DINING END
9'0"

ENTRY

LIVING ROOM
13'0" x 27'2"

CLOSET

HALL

DESIGN FOR A FIVE ROOM HOUSE

LAUNDRY
8'6" x 12'6"

FUEL
7'6" x 13'0"

HEATER
8'6" x 13'0"

STORAGE
10'0" x 13'0"

FRUIT

BATH

BED ROOM
9'6" x 12'0"

CLOS.

BED ROOM
12'0" x 17'0"

CLOS.

BASEMENT FLOOR PLAN   SECOND FLOOR PLAN

SCALE IN FEET OF PLANS & ELEVATIONS

CUBAGE COMPUTATIONS		
HOUSE: BASEMENT & FIRST FLOOR 24' x 29' x 18' = 12,528 CU FT		
HALF WAY BETWEEN PL. & RIDGE 24' x 29' x 9' = 6264 "		
DORMER IN FRONT 4' x 2' x 13' = 104		
" REAR 4' x 2' x 16½' = 132	19,028	
GARAGE: FLOOR TO PLATE 12' x 18' x 7½' = 1620		
HALF WAY PLATE TO RIDGE 12' x 18' x 3' = 648	2268	
TOTAL CU FT	21,296	

EXTERIOR WALLS TO BE BUILT OF HOLLOW BUILDING TILE, WITH RED BRICK TRIM AND WITH WHITE STUCCO, SPATTER DASH FINISH. IN SIDE OF WALLS FURRED AND PLASTERED. ROOF IN VARIEGATED SLATE COLORS. WOOD TRIM GREY. SASH BLUE-GREEN.

18'0"

16'0"

REAR ELEVATION   SIDE ELEVATION

SCALE IN FEET

GEORGE L. EKVALL
ARCHITECT
432 PROVIDENT BLDG
TACOMA WASH.

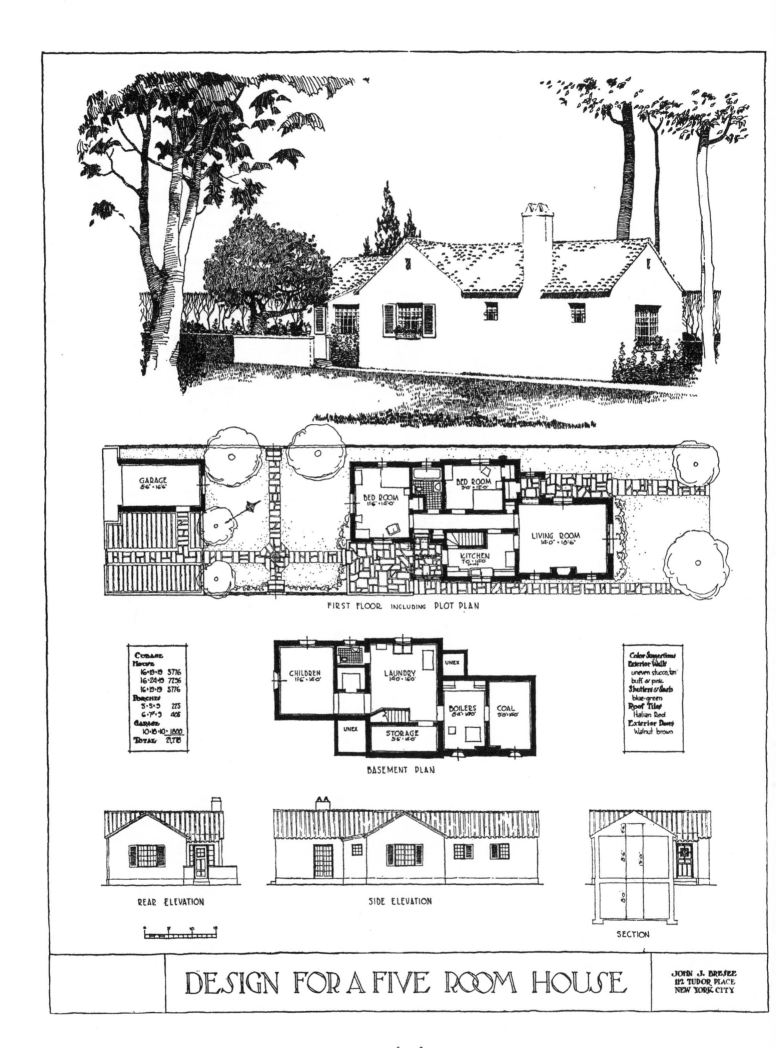

GARAGE
8'6" × 16'6"

FIRST FLOOR INCLUDING PLOT PLAN

BED ROOM
11'6" × 14'0"

BED ROOM
5'0" × 12'0"

KITCHEN
7'0" × 14'0"

LIVING ROOM
14'0" × 18'6"

CUBAGE
House
16·13·13   5776
16·24·19   7296
16·19·19   5776
Porches
5·5·5   225
6·7·9   405
Garage
10·13·10   1800
Total   21,278

CHILDREN
11'6" × 14'0"

LAUNDRY
14'0" × 16'0"

UNEX

UNEX

STORAGE
5'6" × 16'0"

BOILERS
8'4" × 14'0"

COAL
5'8" × 14'0"

BASEMENT PLAN

Color Suggestions
Exterior Walls
uneven stucco, tan
buff or pink
Shutters & Sash
blue-green
Roof Tiles
Italian Red
Exterior Doors
Walnut brown

REAR ELEVATION

SIDE ELEVATION

SECTION

DESIGN FOR A FIVE ROOM HOUSE

JOHN J. BRESEE
112 TUDOR PLACE
NEW YORK CITY

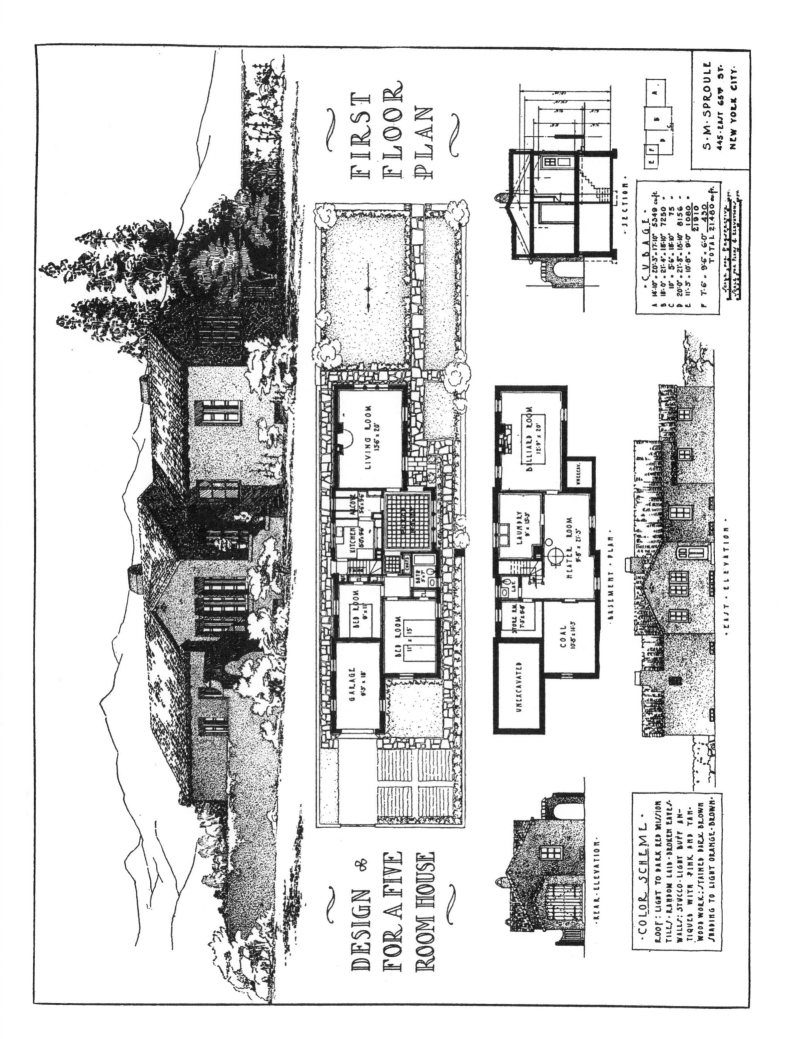

DESIGN &
FOR A FIVE
ROOM HOUSE

FIRST
FLOOR
PLAN

·COLOR·SCHEME·
ROOF: LIGHT TO DARK RED MISSION
TILE/: RANDOM LAID · BROKEN EAVE/·
WALL/: STUCCO · LIGHT BUFF AN-
TIQUED WITH PINK AND TAN.
WOOD WORK: /TAINED DARK BROWN·
/HADING TO LIGHT ORANGE-BROWN·

S·M·SPROULE
445·EAST 65TH ST·
NEW YORK CITY·

·CUBAGE·
A 14'-10" · 20'-3" · 17'-10"   5349 cu.ft.
B 18'-0" · 21'-4" · 18'-10"   7250 ·
C 10' · 5'-6" · 18'-10"   75 ·
D 20'-0" · 21'-8" · 10'-10"   8156 ·
E 11'-5" · 10'-8" · 9'-0"   1080 ·
                              21910
F 7'-6" · 9'-6" · 6'-0"   430 ·
              TOTAL 21,480 cu.ft.

·SECTION·

·BASEMENT·PLAN·

·EAST·ELEVATION·

·REAR·ELEVATION·

LIVING ROOM
15'-6" x 20'

ALCOVE
5'-6" x 6'

KITCHEN
8'-0" x 9'-6"

BED ROOM
9' x 11'

BED ROOM
11' x 15'

GARAGE
9'-5" x 18'

BILLIARD ROOM
12'-9" x 20'

LAUNDRY
9' x 13'-5"

HEATER ROOM
9'-6" x 21'-5"

STORE RM
7'-6" x 6'-6"

COAL
10'-5" x 11'-3"

UNEXCAVATED

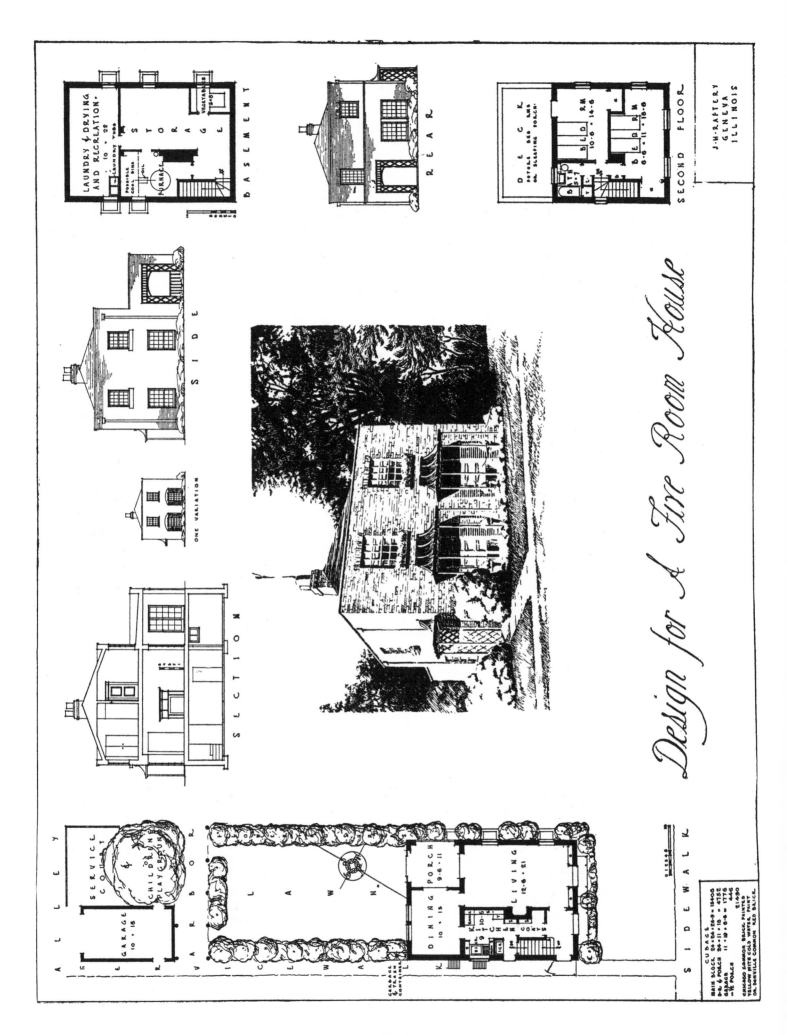

Design for A Five Room House

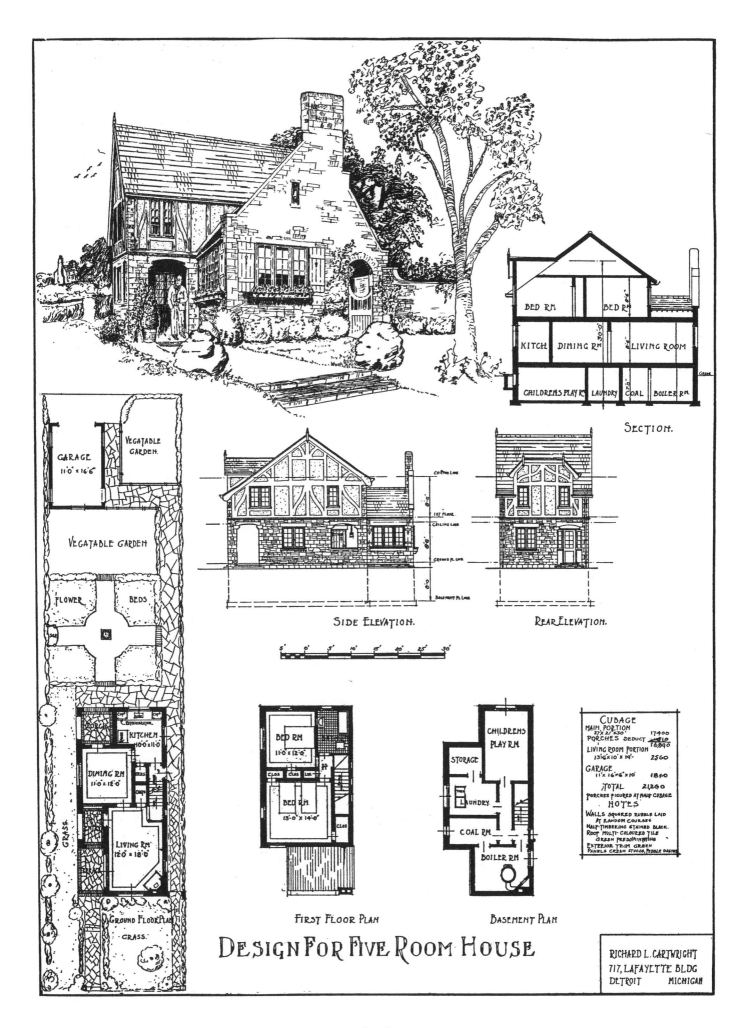

SECTION.

SIDE ELEVATION.   REAR ELEVATION.

GARAGE
11'·0" x 16'·6"

VEGATABLE
GARDEN.

VEGATABLE GARDEN

FLOWER   BEDS

PORCH

KITCHEN
10'·0" x 11'·0"

DINING RM.
11'·0" x 15'·0"

LIVING RM.
12'·0" x 18'·0"

GRASS.

Ground Floor Plan

GRASS.

BED RM.
11'·0" x 12'·0"

CLOS. CLOS. CLOS.

BED RM.
13'·0" x 14'·0"

CLOS

First Floor Plan

CHILDRENS
PLAY RM.

STORAGE

LAUNDRY.

COAL RM.

BOILER RM

Basement Plan

CUBAGE
MAIN PORTION
27' x 21' x 30'   17400
PORCHES DEDUCT   1810
                              16890
LIVING ROOM PORTION
13'·6" x 10' x 19'·   2560
GARAGE
11' x 16'·6" x 10'   1810
TOTAL   21260
PORCHES FIGURED AT HALF CUBAGE
NOTES
WALLS SQUARED RUBBLE LAID
  AT RANDOM COURSES
HALF-TIMBERING STAINED BLACK.
ROOF MULTI-COLOURED TILE
  GREEN PREDOMINATING
EXTERIOR TRIM GREEN
PANELS CREAM STUCCO, PEBBLE DASH

DESIGN FOR FIVE ROOM HOUSE

RICHARD L. CARTWRIGHT
717, LAFAYETTE BLDG
DETROIT   MICHIGAN

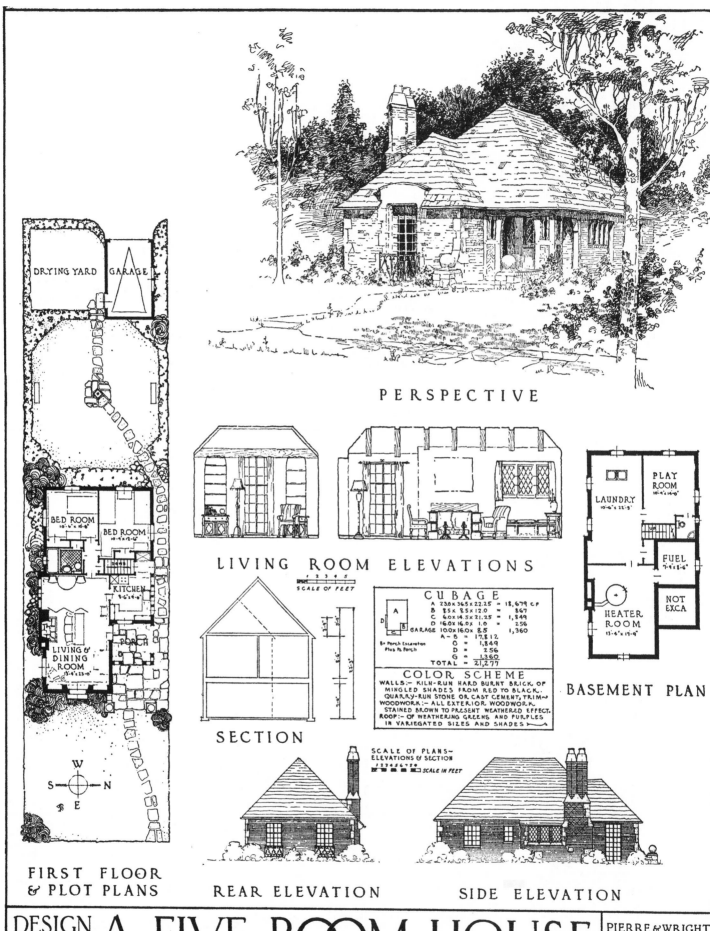

PERSPECTIVE

LIVING ROOM ELEVATIONS

DRYING YARD   GARAGE

BED ROOM
10'-6" x 10'-0"

BED ROOM
10'-4" x 12'-6"

KITCHEN
9'-6" x 9'-0"

PORCH

LIVING &
DINING
ROOM
15'-0" x 23'-0"

W
S   N
E

SECTION

CUBAGE

A 23.0 x 36.5 x 22.25 = 18,679 c.f.
B 8.5 x 8.5 x 12.0 = 867
C 6.0 x 14.5 x 21.25 = 1,849
D 16.0 x 16.0 x 1.0 = 256
GARAGE 10.0 x 16.0 x 8.5 = 1,360

A - B   17,812
C   1,849
D   256
G   1,360
TOTAL = 21,277

B = Porch Excavation
Plus ½ Porch

COLOR SCHEME

WALLS:— KILN-RUN HARD BURNT BRICK OF
MINGLED SHADES FROM RED TO BLACK.
QUARRY-RUN STONE OR CAST CEMENT, TRIM~
WOODWORK:— ALL EXTERIOR WOODWORK
STAINED BROWN TO PRESENT WEATHERED EFFECT.
ROOF:— OF WEATHERING GREENS AND PURPLES
IN VARIEGATED SIZES AND SHADES ~

SCALE OF FEET
1 2 3 4 5

PLAY
ROOM
10'-6" x 14'-0"

LAUNDRY
10'-6" x 22'-9"

FUEL
7'-6" x 8'-6"

NOT
EXCA

HEATER
ROOM
13'-4" x 17'-9"

BASEMENT PLAN

SCALE OF PLANS~
ELEVATIONS & SECTION
1 2 3 4 5 6 7 8 9   SCALE IN FEET

FIRST FLOOR
& PLOT PLANS

REAR ELEVATION

SIDE ELEVATION

DESIGN FOR A FIVE ROOM HOUSE

PIERRE & WRIGHT
ARCHITECTS
1133 HUME MANSUR BUILDING
INDIANAPOLIS, INDIANA

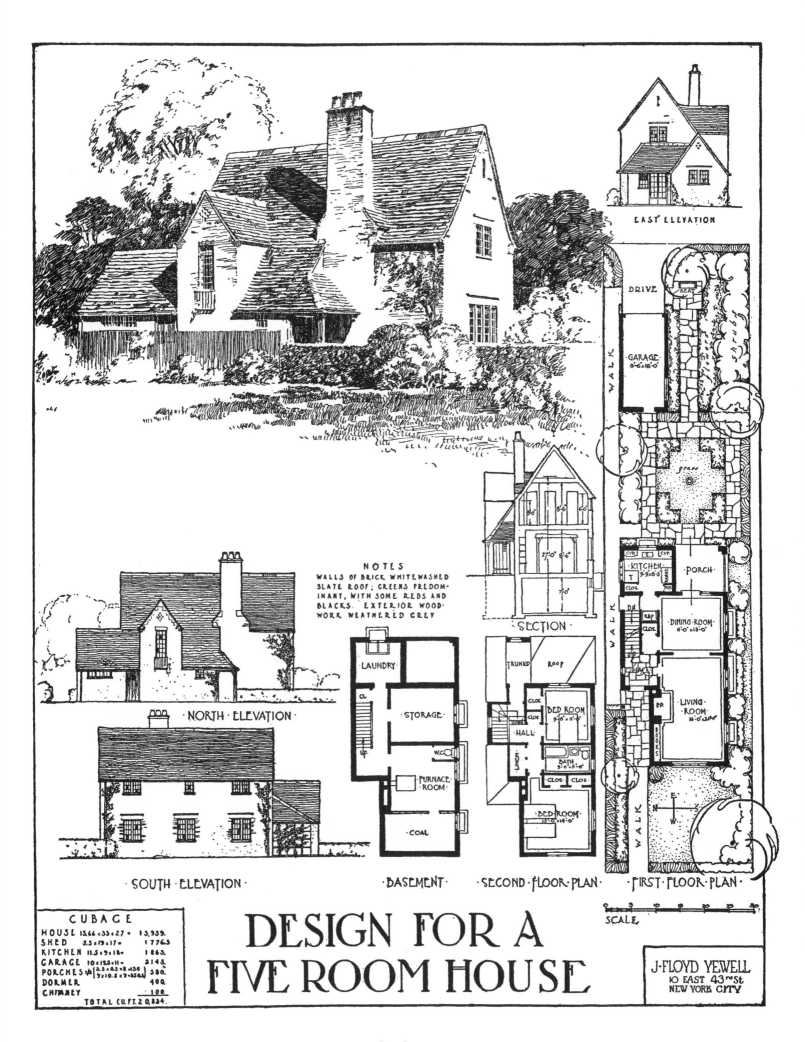

EAST ELEVATION

NOTES
WALLS OF BRICK WHITEWASHED
SLATE ROOF; GREENS PREDOM-
INANT, WITH SOME REDS AND
BLACKS. EXTERIOR WOOD-
WORK WEATHERED GREY

SECTION

NORTH ELEVATION

SOUTH ELEVATION

BASEMENT

SECOND FLOOR PLAN

FIRST FLOOR PLAN

SCALE

CUBAGE		
HOUSE 15.66×33×27 =	13,939.
SHED 5.5×19×17 =	1776.3
KITCHEN 11.5×9×18 =	1863.
GARAGE 10×12.5×11 =	2145.
PORCHES A 3.5×45×9.454	580.
5×10.5×9×450	
DORMER	400.
CHIMNEY	100.
TOTAL CU.FT.	20,824.

DESIGN FOR A FIVE ROOM HOUSE

J·FLOYD YEWELL
10 EAST 43RD St
NEW YORK CITY

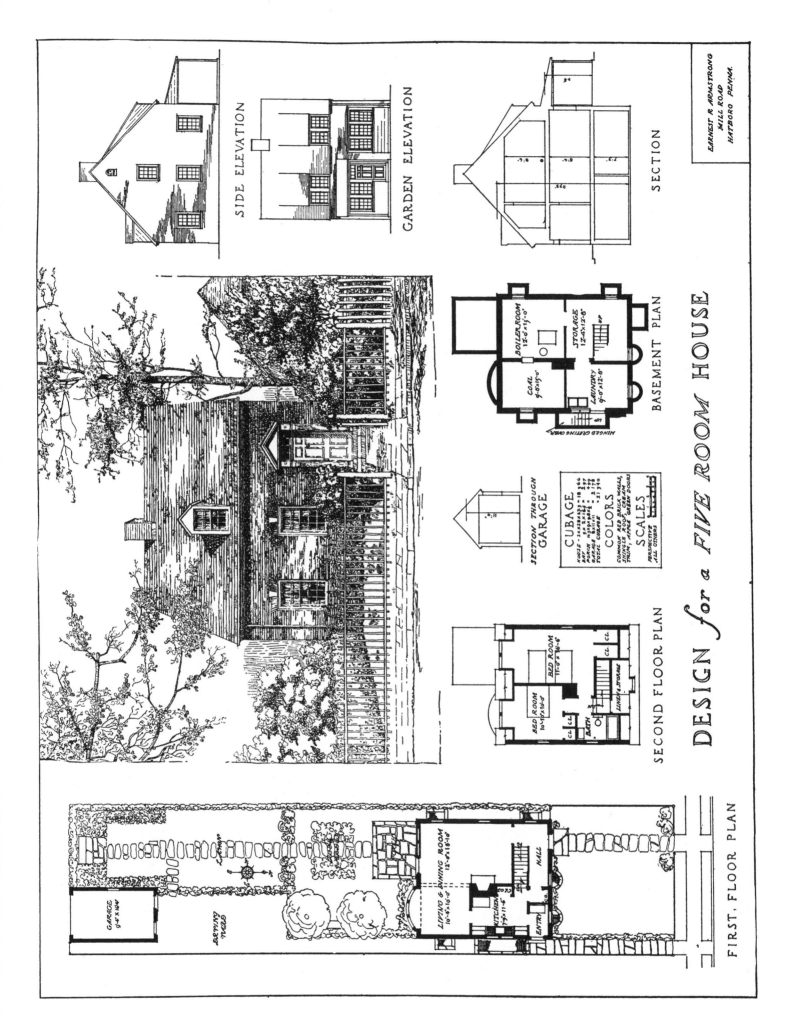

SIDE ELEVATION

GARDEN ELEVATION

SECTION

EARNEST R ARMSTRONG
MILL ROAD
HATBORO PENNA.

BASEMENT PLAN

BOILER ROOM
12'-6"×13'-0"

COAL
9'-6"×13'-0"

STORAGE
12'-4"×12'-6"

LAUNDRY
9'-0"×12'-6"

HINGED GRATING OVER

SECTION THROUGH GARAGE

CUBAGE

COLORS

COMMON RED BRICK WALLS, SHINGLE ROOF, CREAM TRIM, APPLE GREEN DOORS

SCALES

PERSPECTIVE
ALL OTHERS

SECOND FLOOR PLAN

BED ROOM
10'-4"×16'-0"

BED ROOM
11'-0"×16'-6"

CL
CL
CL
CL
BATH
LINEN & STORAGE

FIRST FLOOR PLAN

GARAGE
9'-4"×16'-6"

BURNING YARD

LIVING & DINING ROOM
12'-4"×18'-10"

HALL
KITCHEN
ENTRY

DESIGN for a FIVE ROOM HOUSE

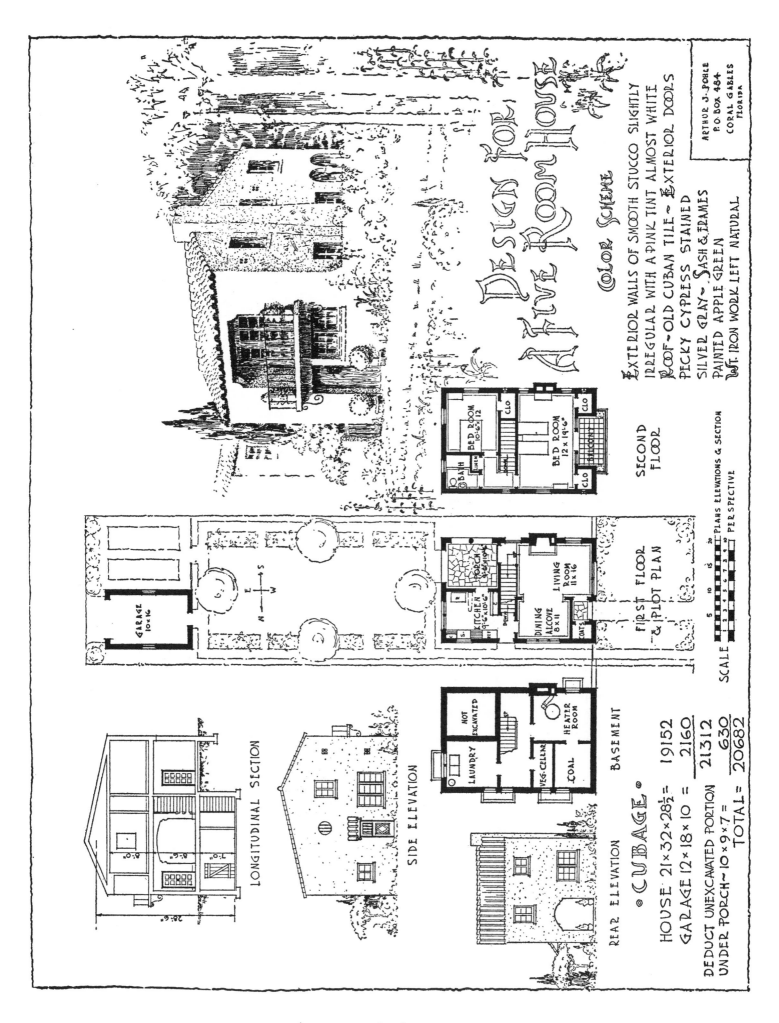

A DESIGN FOR A FIVE ROOM HOUSE

ARTHUR J. POHLE
P.O. BOX 484
CORAL GABLES
FLORIDA

COLOR SCHEME

EXTERIOR WALLS OF SMOOTH STUCCO SLIGHTLY
IRREGULAR WITH A PINK TINT ALMOST WHITE
ROOF~OLD CUBAN TILE~ EXTERIOR DOORS
PECKY CYPRESS STAINED
SILVER GRAY~ SASH & FRAMES
PAINTED APPLE GREEN
WT. IRON WORK LEFT NATURAL

SECOND FLOOR

BED ROOM 10'-6"×12
BED ROOM 12×14'-6"
BATH
CLO
CLO
BALCONY

FIRST FLOOR & PLOT PLAN

GARAGE 10×16
KITCHEN 9'-6"×10'-6"
PORCH
LIVING ROOM 11×16
DINING ALCOVE 8×11
COATS

SCALE
5   10   15   20
1 2 3 4 5 6 7 8   10   PLANS ELEVATIONS & SECTION
1 2 3 4   PERSPECTIVE

BASEMENT

NOT EXCAVATED
LAUNDRY
HEATER ROOM
VEG·CELLAR
COAL

REAR ELEVATION

LONGITUDINAL SECTION

SIDE ELEVATION

CUBAGE

HOUSE 21×32×28½ = 19152
GARAGE 12×18×10 = 2160
                  21312
DEDUCT UNEXCAVATED PORTION
UNDER PORCH~10×9×7 =   630
          TOTAL = 20682

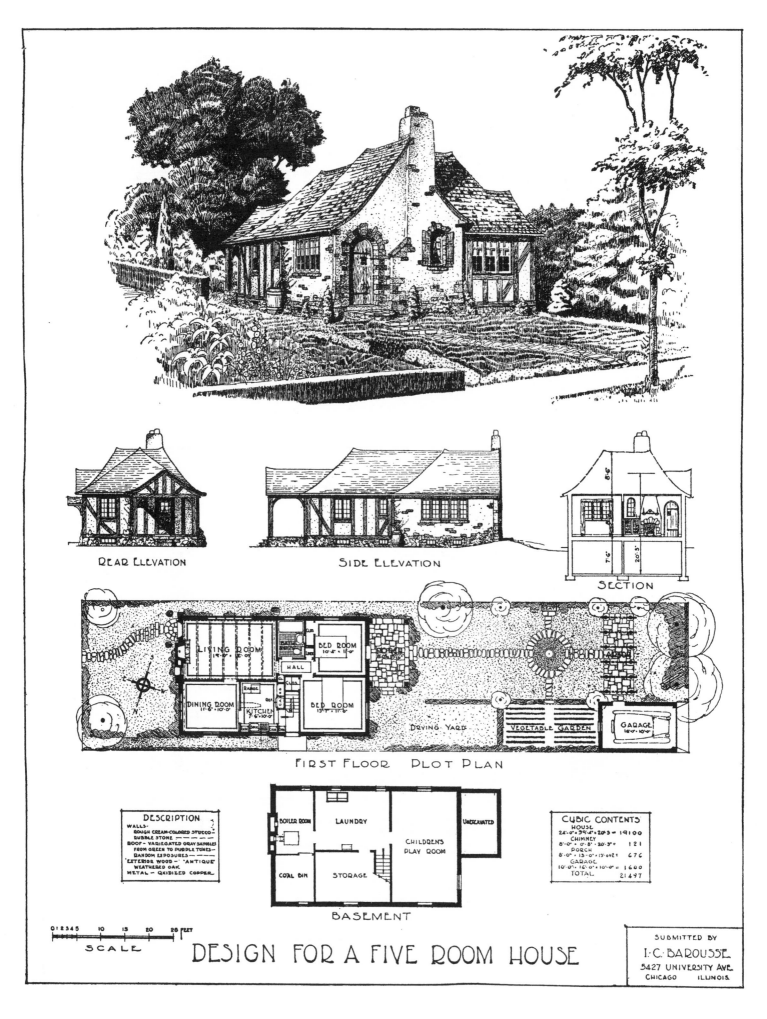

REAR ELEVATION

SIDE ELEVATION

SECTION

LIVING ROOM

BED ROOM

HALL

DINING ROOM

KITCHEN

BED ROOM

PORCH

DRYING YARD

VEGETABLE GARDEN

GARAGE

FIRST FLOOR PLOT PLAN

BOILER ROOM

LAUNDRY

UNEXCAVATED

CHILDREN'S PLAY ROOM

COAL BIN

STORAGE

BASEMENT

DESCRIPTION
WALLS–
ROUGH CREAM-COLORED STUCCO–
RUBBLE STONE–
ROOF– VARIEGATED GRAY SHINGLES
FROM GREEN TO PURPLE TONES–
RANDOM EXPOSURES—
EXTERIOR WOOD–'ANTIQUE'
WEATHERED OAK–
METAL– OXIDIZED COPPER–

CUBIC CONTENTS
HOUSE 24'-0" x 39'-4" x 20'-3" =	19100
CHIMNEY 8'-0" x 0'-8" x 20'-3" =	121
PORCH 8'-0" x 13'-0" x 13'-0" ÷2 =	676
GARAGE 10'-0" x 16'-0" x 10'-0" =	1600
TOTAL	21497

0 1 2 3 4 5 10 15 20 25 FEET
SCALE

DESIGN FOR A FIVE ROOM HOUSE

SUBMITTED BY
I. C. BAROUSSE
5427 UNIVERSITY AVE.
CHICAGO   ILLINOIS

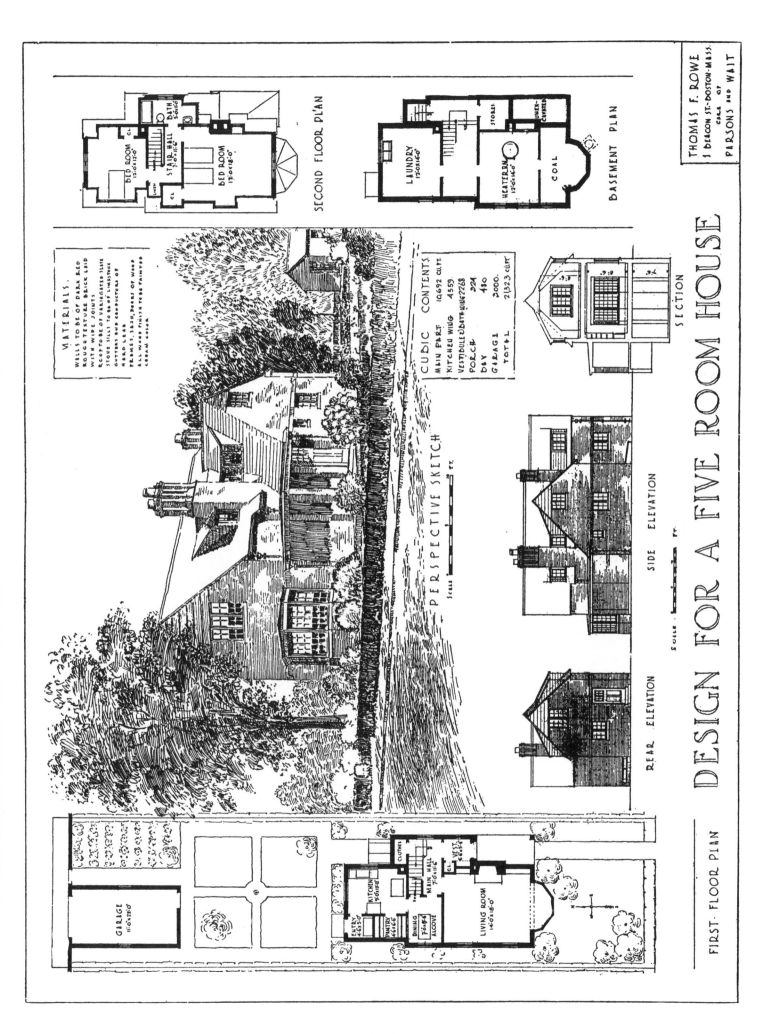

SECOND FLOOR PLAN

BED ROOM
13'-0"x12'-0"

STAIR HALL
7'-0"x11'-0"

BED ROOM
13'-0"x16'-0"

BATH
9'x10'-0"

CL

CL

BASEMENT PLAN

LAUNDRY
13'-0"x14'-0"

STORE

UNEX-
CAVATED

HEAT RM
13'-0"x14'-0"

COAL

MATERIALS.

WALLS TO BE OF DARK RED
ROUGH TEXTURE BRICK LAID
WITH WIPE JOINTS

ROOF TO BE OF VARIEGATED SLATE
STONE SILLS TO BE OF LIMESTONE

GUTTERS AND CONDUCTORS OF
HARD LEAD

FRAMES, SASH, DOORS OF WOOD
ALL WOOD FINISH TO BE PAINTED
CREAM COLOR

CUBIC CONTENTS

MAIN PART   10692 CU.FT.
KITCHEN WING   4559
VESTIBULE & BATH WING 2268
PORCH   324
BAY   480
GARAGE   3000
TOTAL   21323 CU.FT.

PERSPECTIVE SKETCH

SCALE   FT.

SECTION

REAR ELEVATION

SIDE ELEVATION

SCALE   FT.

THOMAS F. ROWE
1 BEACON ST. BOSTON MASS.
CARE OF
PARSONS AND WAIT

DESIGN FOR A FIVE ROOM HOUSE

FIRST FLOOR PLAN

GARAGE
11'-0"x20'-0"

KITCHEN
15'-0"x15'-0"

ENTRY
4'-6"x5'-0"

PANTRY
4'-6"x6'-6"

DINING
ALCOVE
7'-6"x6'-6"

MAIN HALL
7'-0"x11'-0"

CLOTHES

CL

VEST.
6'-6"x6'-6"

LIVING ROOM
14'-0"x16'-0"

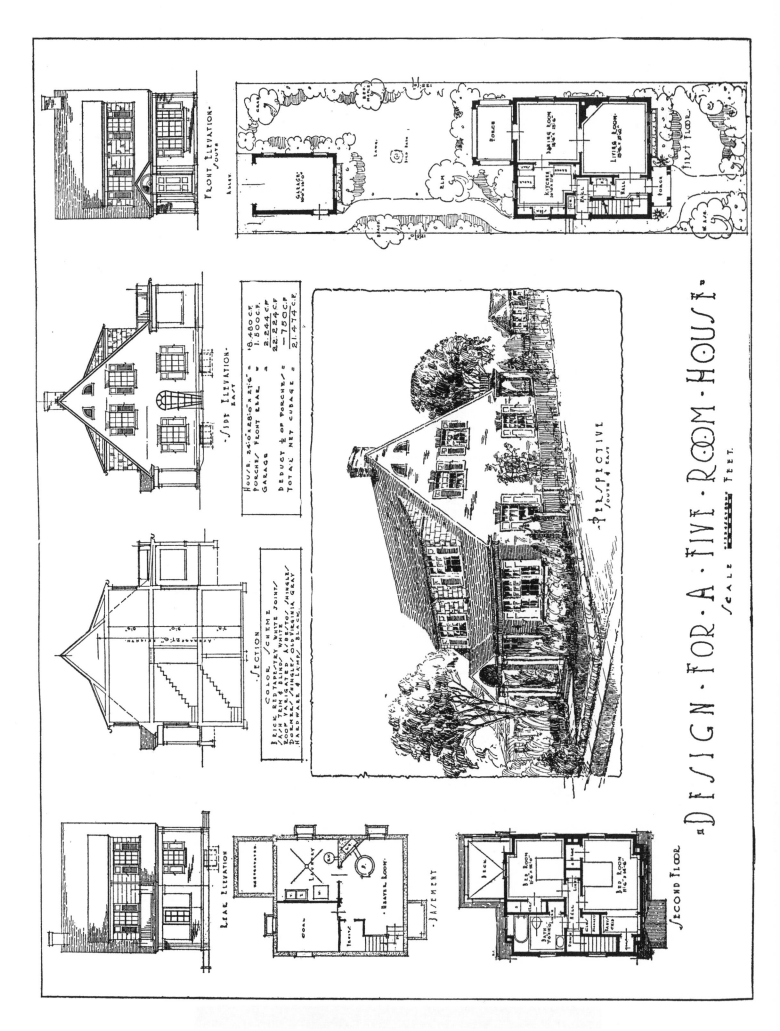

FRONT ELEVATION.
SOUTH.

FIRST FLOOR.

SIDE ELEVATION.
EAST.

HOUSE: 24'-0" x 28'-0" x 21'-6" = 18.480 C.F.
PORCHE: FRONT ELEV. = 1.500 C.F.
GARAGE = 2.244 C.F.
= 22.224 C.F.
DEDUCT ½ OF PORCHES = 750 C.F.
TOTAL NET CUBAGE = 21.474 C.F.

COLOR SCHEME
BRICK: RED TAPESTRY WHITE JOINT/
SASH TRIM & BLIND/ WHITE
ROOF VARIEGATED ASBESTOS SHINGLE/
DRAIN BACK SHINGLE/ OLD VIRGINIA GRAY
HARDWARE & LAMP/ BLACK.

SECTION.

PERSPECTIVE
SOUTH & EAST.

REAR ELEVATION.

BASEMENT.

SECOND FLOOR.

DESIGN · FOR · A · FIVE · ROOM · HOUSE.
SCALE FEET.

[80]

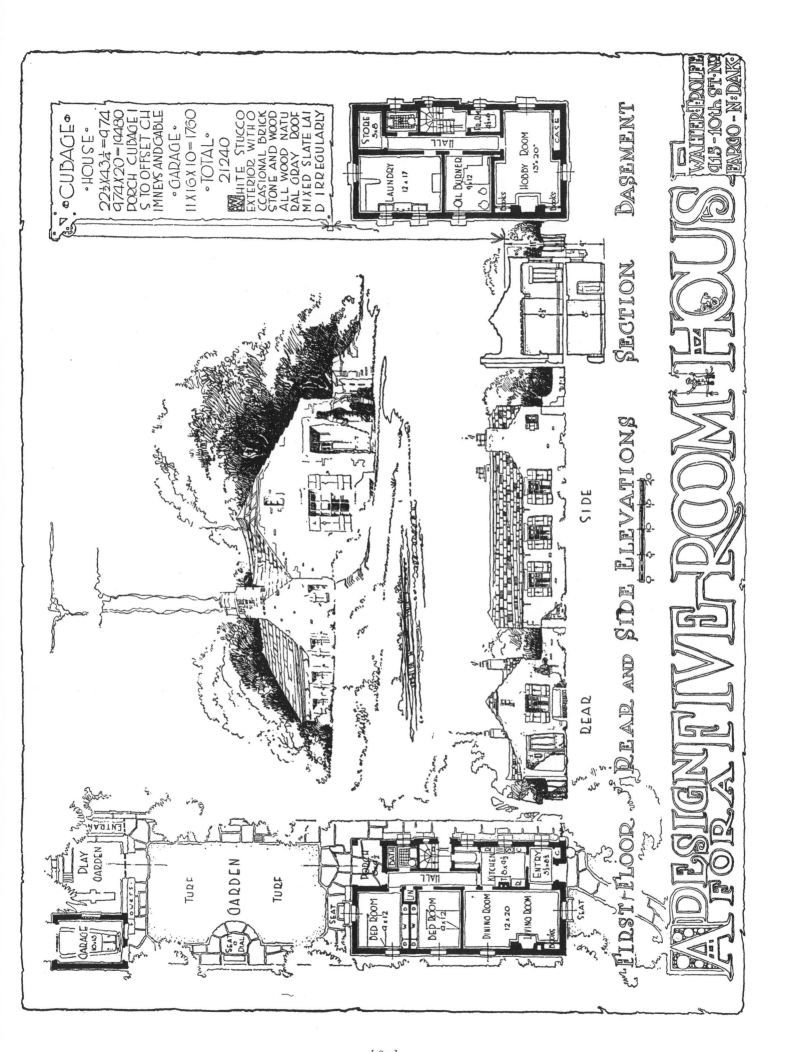

A DESIGN FOR A LIVING·ROOM·HOUSE

WATERHOUSE
415·10th·St·No.
FARGO·N·DAK.

FIRST-FLOOR, REAR and SIDE ELEVATIONS·· SECTION·· BASEMENT

·CUBAGE·
·HOUSE·
22½x43½=974
974x20=19480
PORCH CUBAGE I
S TO OFFSET CH
IMNEYS AND GABLE
·GARAGE·
11x16x10=1760
·TOTAL·
21240

WHITE STUCCO
EXTERIOR WITH O
CCASIONAL BRICK
STONE AND WOOD
ALL WOOD NATU
RAL GRAY ROOF
MIXED SLATE LAI
D IRREGULARLY

BASEMENT

STORE
5x8
LAUNDRY
12x17
OIL BURNER
9x12
HALL
HOBBY ROOM
15x20"
CASE
BOOKS
BOOKS

SIDE

REAR

GARAGE
10x15
ENTRANCE
PLAY GARDEN

TURF
GARDEN
TURF

SEAT
DIAL

OVER

SEAT
BED ROOM
9x12
UN
D W
D W
BED ROOM
9x12
DINING ROOM
12x20
LIVING ROOM
PORCH
HALL
KITCHEN
18x9½
ENTRY
5½x6½
SEAT
BOOKS

[81]

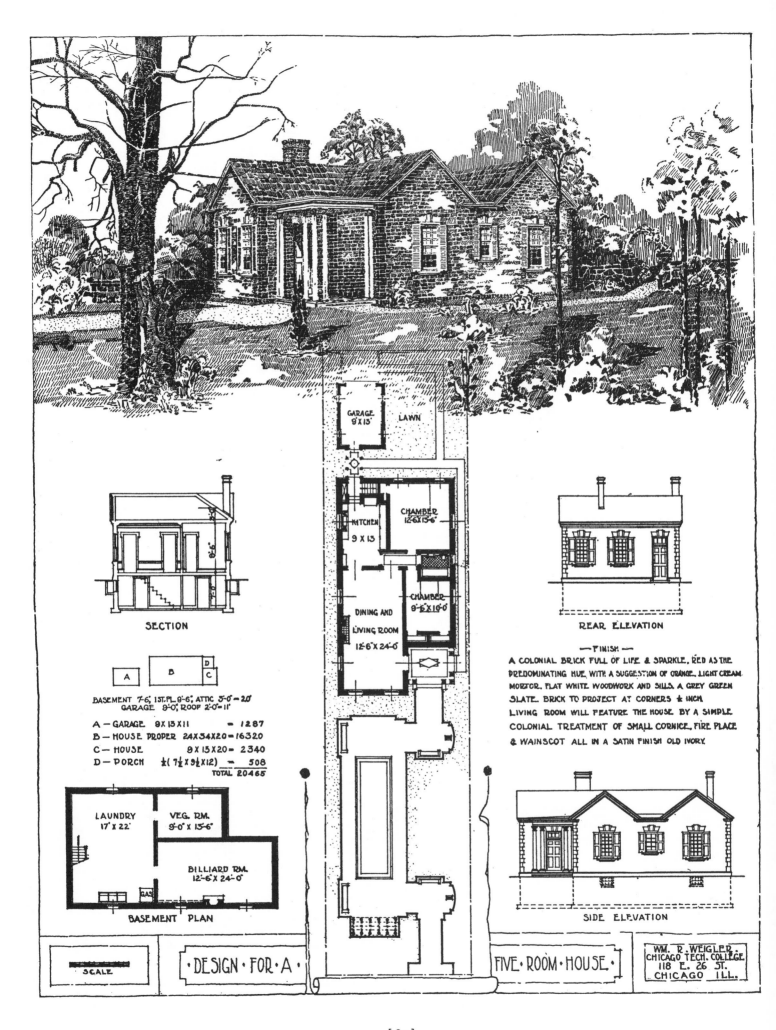

SECTION

BASEMENT 7'-6", 1ST FL. 9'-6", ATTIC 5'-0" = 20'
GARAGE 9'-0", ROOF 2'-0" = 11'

A — GARAGE   9 X 13 X 11   = 1287
B — HOUSE PROPER 24 X 34 X 20 = 16320
C — HOUSE   9 X 13 X 20   = 2340
D — PORCH   ½(7½ X 9½ X 12) = 508
                    TOTAL 20465

LAUNDRY
17' X 22'

VEG. RM.
9'-0" X 15'-6"

BILLIARD RM.
12'-6" X 24'-0"

BASEMENT PLAN

GARAGE
9' X 13'   LAWN

CHAMBER
12'-6" X 15'-6"

KITCHEN
9 X 13

CHAMBER
9'-6" X 10'-6"

DINING AND
LIVING ROOM
12'-6" X 24'-0"

REAR ELEVATION

— FINISH —

A COLONIAL BRICK FULL OF LIFE & SPARKLE, RED AS THE
PREDOMINATING HUE WITH A SUGGESTION OF ORANGE, LIGHT CREAM
MORTAR, FLAT WHITE WOODWORK AND SILLS A GREY GREEN
SLATE. BRICK TO PROJECT AT CORNERS ¼ INCH
LIVING ROOM WILL FEATURE THE HOUSE BY A SIMPLE
COLONIAL TREATMENT OF SMALL CORNICE, FIRE PLACE
& WAINSCOT ALL IN A SATIN FINISH OLD IVORY

SIDE ELEVATION

SCALE

·DESIGN·FOR·A·   ·FIVE·ROOM·HOUSE·

WM. R. WEIGLER.
CHICAGO TECH. COLLEGE
118 E. 26 ST.
CHICAGO ILL.

DESIGN FOR A SIX ROOM HOUSE.

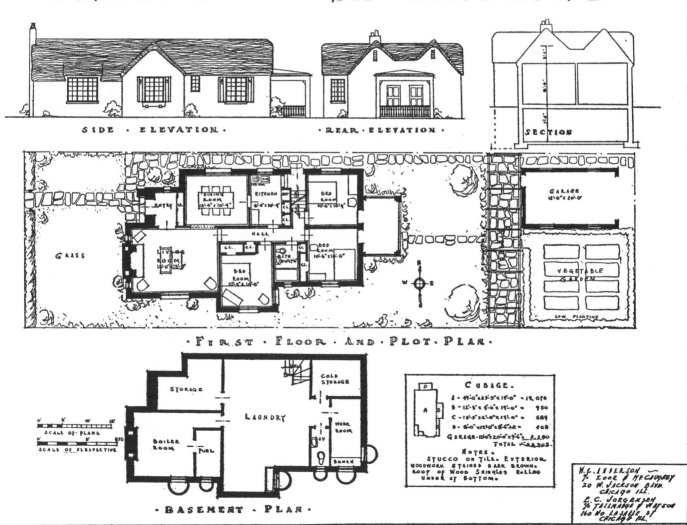

· SIDE · ELEVATION ·   · REAR · ELEVATION ·   · SECTION ·

· FIRST · FLOOR · AND · PLOT · PLAN ·

· BASEMENT · PLAN ·

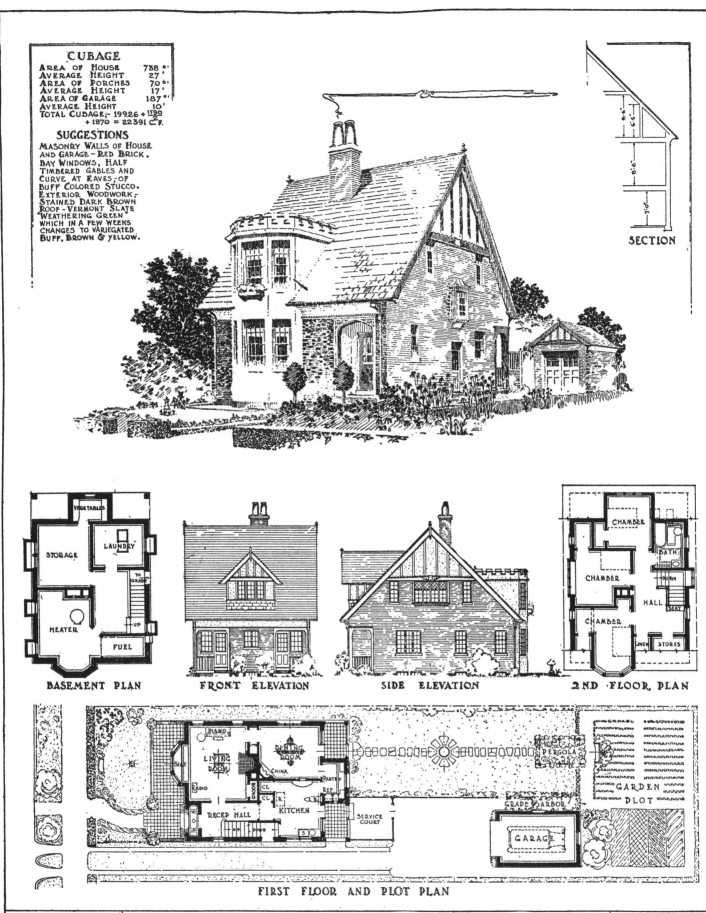

CUBAGE
AREA OF HOUSE   738 ▫"
AVERAGE HEIGHT   27 '
AREA OF PORCHES   70 ▫"
AVERAGE HEIGHT   17 '
AREA OF GARAGE   187 ▫"
AVERAGE HEIGHT   10 '
TOTAL CUBAGE:- 19926 + 1199
    + 1870 = 22391 C.F.

SUGGESTIONS
MASONRY WALLS OF HOUSE
AND GARAGE - RED BRICK.
BAY WINDOWS, HALF
TIMBERED GABLES AND
CURVE AT EAVES - OF
BUFF COLORED STUCCO.
EXTERIOR WOODWORK -
STAINED DARK BROWN
ROOF - VERMONT SLATE
"WEATHERING GREEN"
WHICH IN A FEW WEEKS
CHANGES TO VARIEGATED
BUFF, BROWN & YELLOW.

SECTION

BASEMENT PLAN

FRONT ELEVATION

SIDE ELEVATION

2ND FLOOR PLAN

FIRST FLOOR AND PLOT PLAN

SCALE OF PLANS
& ELEVATIONS
5   10   15

DESIGN FOR A SIX ROOM HOVSE

WILLIAM E. ASH
35 WOODS AVE
WEST SOMERVILLE
MASS.

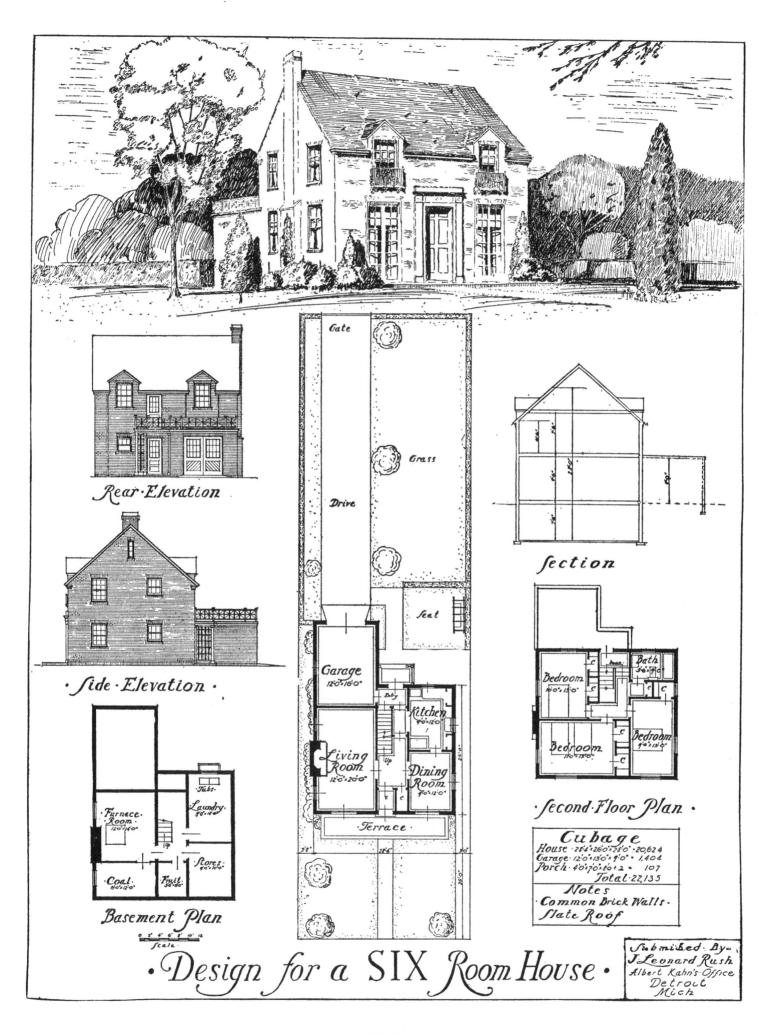

Rear Elevation

Section

Side Elevation

Gate

Grass

Drive

Seat

Garage
12'0"·16'0"

Living
Room
12'0"·20'0"

Kitchen
9'0"·12'0"

Dining
Room
9'0"·12'0"

Terrace

Bedroom
10'0"·13'0"

Bath
5'6"·9'0"

Bedroom
9'0"·15'0"

Bedroom
11'0"·15'0"

Second Floor Plan

Basement Plan

Furnace
Room
12'0"·14'0"

Laundry
9'0"·14

Tubs.

Stores.
9'0"·10'0"

Coal
6'0"·12'0"

Fruit
5'6"·6'0"

Scale

Cubage
House 28'4"·26'0"·28'0"·20,624
Garage 12'0"·13'0"·9'0"· 1,404
Porch 4'0"·7'0"·8'0"÷2   107
Total 22,135
Notes
Common Brick Walls.
Slate Roof

Submitted By
J. Leonard Rush
Albert Kahn's Office
Detroit
Mich

·Design for a SIX Room House·

—SOUTH ELEVATION—

SCALE
0   5   10   15   20   25   30   35

—SECTION—

—EAST ELEVATION—

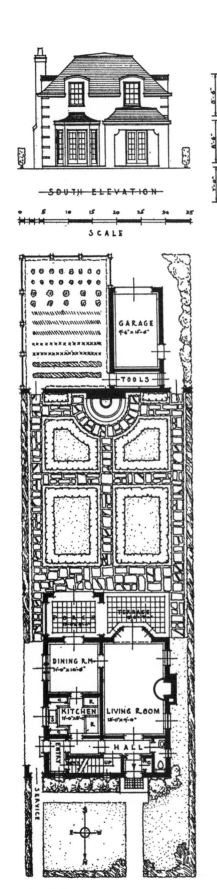

GARAGE
9'-6" x 15'-6"

TOOLS

DINING RM.
11'-0" x 10'-6"

KITCHEN
11'-0" x 8'-6"

LIVING ROOM
18'-0" x 14'-0"

PORCH

TERRACE

HALL

ENTRY   UP

SERVICE

—FIRST FLOOR & PLOT PLAN—

·DESIGN·FOR·A·SIX·ROOM·HOUSE·

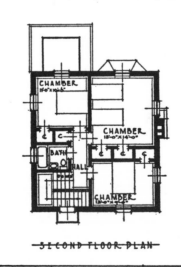

CHAMBER
16'-0" x 10'-6"

CHAMBER
18'-0" x 14'-0"

BATH

HALL

CHAMBER
18'-0" x 14'-0"

—SECOND FLOOR PLAN—

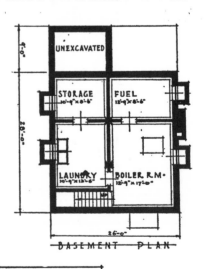

UNEXCAVATED

STORAGE
10'-9" x 8'-6"

FUEL
12'-9" x 8'-6"

LAUNDRY
10'-9" x 13'-6"

BOILER RM.
12'-9" x 17'-0"

—BASEMENT PLAN—

CUBAGE			NOTES
HOUSE	26×28×26 =	18,928	HOUSE FINISHED IN CREAM
PORCH	12.5×9×10.5 =	1,181	STUCCO ON HOLLOW TILE
BAY	2×7×10 =	140	COPPER DECKS, GUTTERS &
AREAS	4×4.5×2×3 =	108	FLASHING·ALL EXTERIOR
GARAGE	11×21×11 =	2,541	WOOD TRIM, SASH & DOORS
TOTAL CU. FEET		22,898	PAINTED BOTTLE GREEN

SUBMITTED BY
THOMAS W. COOPER
ARCHITECT
BLACK MOUNTAIN, NORTH CAR.

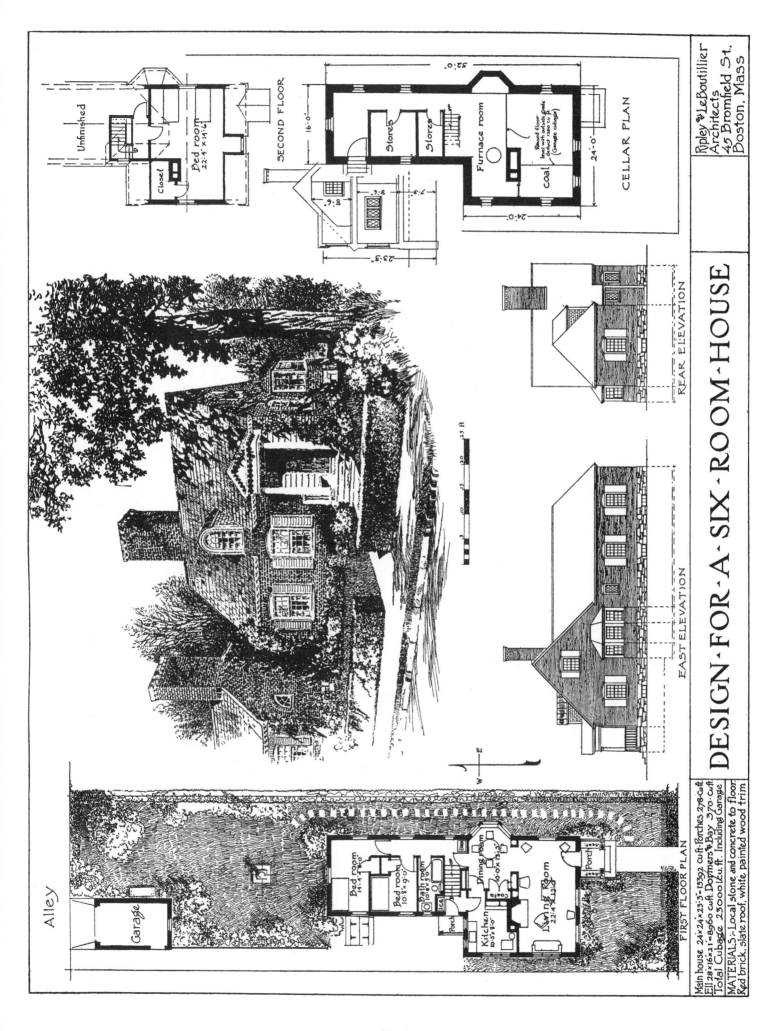

Unfinished

Closet

Bed room
22'4" x 14'6"

SECOND FLOOR

Stores

Stores

Furnace room

Raised floor level with outside grade (Garage cubage)

Coal

CELLAR PLAN

REAR ELEVATION

EAST ELEVATION

Alley

Garage

Bed room
14'4" x

Bed room
10'8" x 9'0"

Bath room
10' x 5'0"

Dining room
10'0" x 12'

Kitchen
10'3" x 8'0"

Living Room
22'4" x 12'

Porch

FIRST FLOOR PLAN

Ripley & LeBoutillier
Architects
45 Bromfield St.
Boston, Mass

DESIGN·FOR·A·SIX·ROOM·HOUSE

Main house 24'x24'x23'-3"·13392 cu.ft. Porches 278 cu.ft.
Ell 28'x16'x21=8960 cu.ft. Dormers & Bay 370 cu.ft.
Total Cubage 25000 cu.ft. Including Garage
MATERIALS:- Local stone and concrete to floor
Red brick, slate roof, white painted wood trim

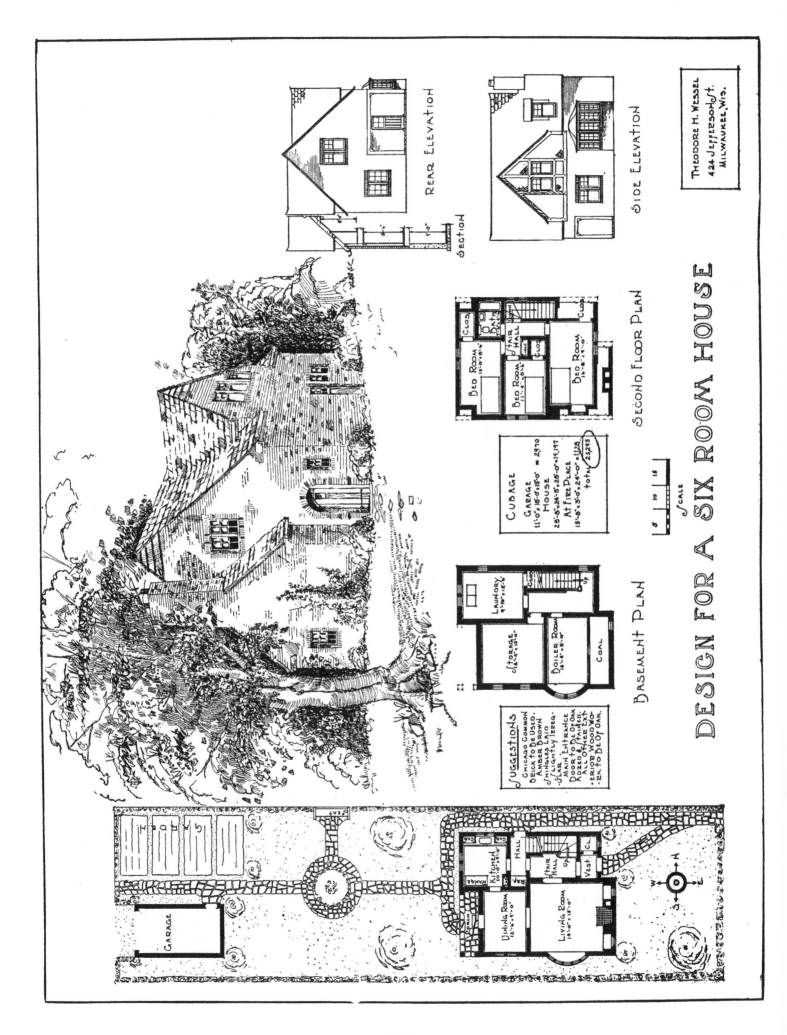

REAR ELEVATION

SIDE ELEVATION

SECTION

THEODORE H. WESSEL
424 JEFFERSON St.
MILWAUKEE, WIS.

SECOND FLOOR PLAN

BED ROOM

STAIR HALL

BED ROOM

CLOS.

CLOS.

CLOS.

BASEMENT PLAN

LAUNDRY

STORAGE

BOILER ROOM

COAL

UP

CUBAGE
GARAGE
11'-0"x16'-0"x15'-0" = 2370
HOUSE
28'-6"x24'-6"x25'-0" = 19,197
AT FIRE PLACE
15'-6"x3'-6"x24'-0" = 1128
total 23,295

SCALE
5 10 15

SUGGESTIONS
CHICAGO COMMON
BRICK TO BE USED.
AMBER BROWN
SHINGLES LAID
SLIGHTLY IRREG-
-ULAR
MAIN ENTRANCE
DOOR TO BE OF OAK
ADZED & STAINED
ALL OTHER EXT-
-ERIOR WOOD WO-
-RK TO BE OF OAK.

GARAGE

KITCHEN

RANGE

HALL

DINING ROOM

STAIR HALL

UP

VEST.

LIVING ROOM

VEST. CL.

PORCH

N
W E
S

DESIGN FOR A SIX ROOM HOUSE

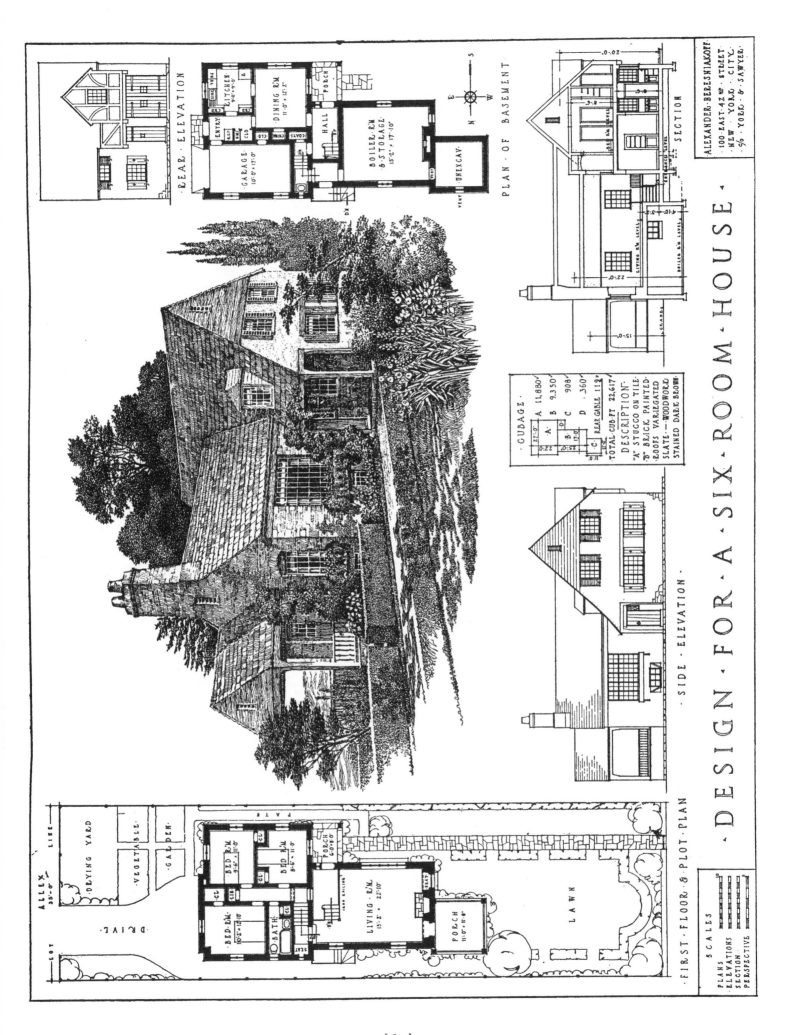

REAR · ELEVATION ·

KITCHEN
9'·0"·9'·0"

DINING · RM
11'·0"·12'·2"

ENTRY

GARAGE
10'·0"·17'·0"

HALL

PORCH

PLAN · OF · BASEMENT

BOILER · RM
& · STORAGE
15'·2"·17'·10"

UNEXCAV.

SECTION

ALEXANDER · BERESNIAKOFF
· 100 · EAST · 42ND · STREET ·
· NEW · YORK · CITY ·
· % · YORK · & · SAWYER ·

· CUBAGE ·

A	11,880	
B	9,350	
C	908	
D	360	

TOTAL · CUB · FT · 22,617

· DESCRIPTION ·
"A" STUCCO ON TILE ·
"B" BRICK PAINTED ·
ROOFS VARIEGATED ·
SLATE — WOODWORK
STAINED DARK BROWN ·

· SIDE · ELEVATION ·

ALLEY
35'·0"

DRYING · YARD

VEGETABLE

GARDEN

DRIVE

BED · RM
9'·6"·11'·0"

BED · RM
8'·6"·11'·0"

PORCH
6'·0"·6'·0"

BED · RM
10'·2"·12'·0"

BATH

SEAT

LIVING · RM
15'·2"·22'·10"

PORCH
11'·0"·6'·0"

PATIO

LAWN

· FIRST · FLOOR · & · PLOT · PLAN ·

· DESIGN · FOR · A · SIX · ROOM · HOUSE ·

· SCALES ·
PLANS
ELEVATIONS
SECTION
PERSPECTIVE

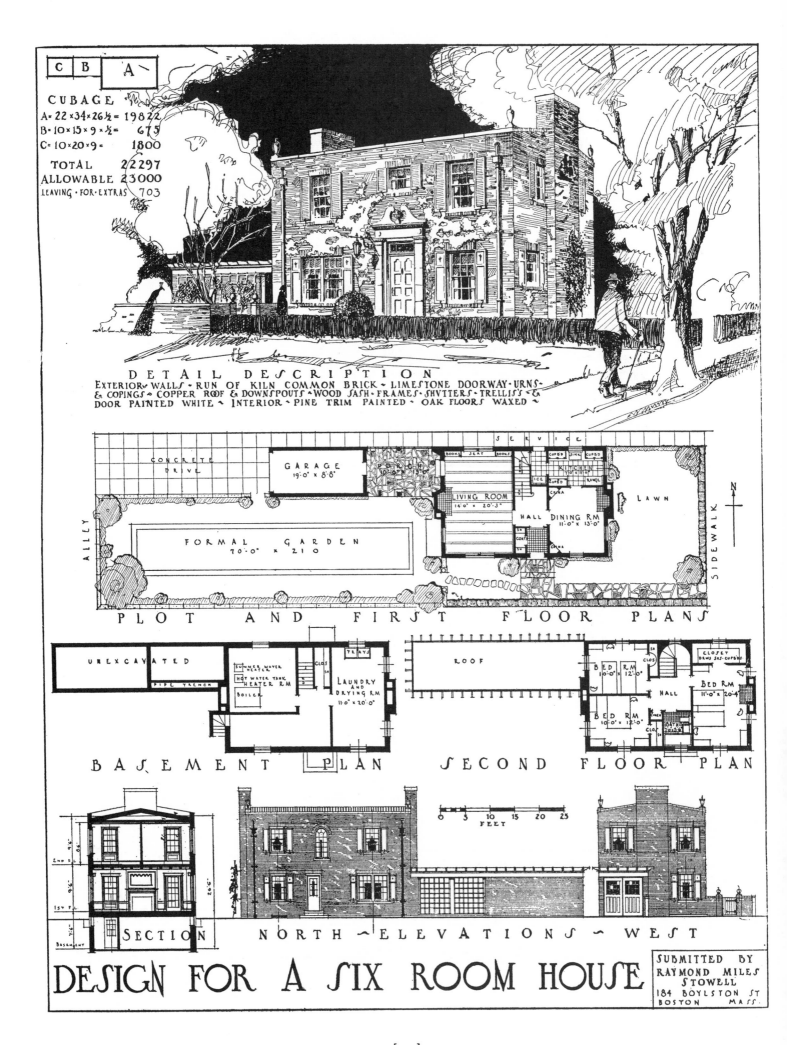

C B A

CUBAGE
A = 22 × 34 × 26½ = 19822
B = 10 × 15 × 9 × ½ = 675
C = 10 × 20 × 9 = 1800

TOTAL 22297
ALLOWABLE 23000
LEAVING · FOR · EXTRAS 703

DETAIL DESCRIPTION
EXTERIOR WALLS · RUN OF KILN COMMON BRICK · LIMESTONE DOORWAY · URNS ·
& COPINGS · COPPER ROOF & DOWNSPOUTS · WOOD SASH FRAMES · SHVTTERS · TRELLIS · &
DOOR PAINTED WHITE · INTERIOR · PINE TRIM PAINTED · OAK FLOORS WAXED ~

PLOT AND FIRST FLOOR PLANS

BASEMENT PLAN — SECOND FLOOR PLAN

SECTION — NORTH ~ ELEVATIONS ~ WEST

DESIGN FOR A SIX ROOM HOUSE

SUBMITTED BY
RAYMOND MILES
STOWELL
184 BOYLSTON ST
BOSTON MASS.

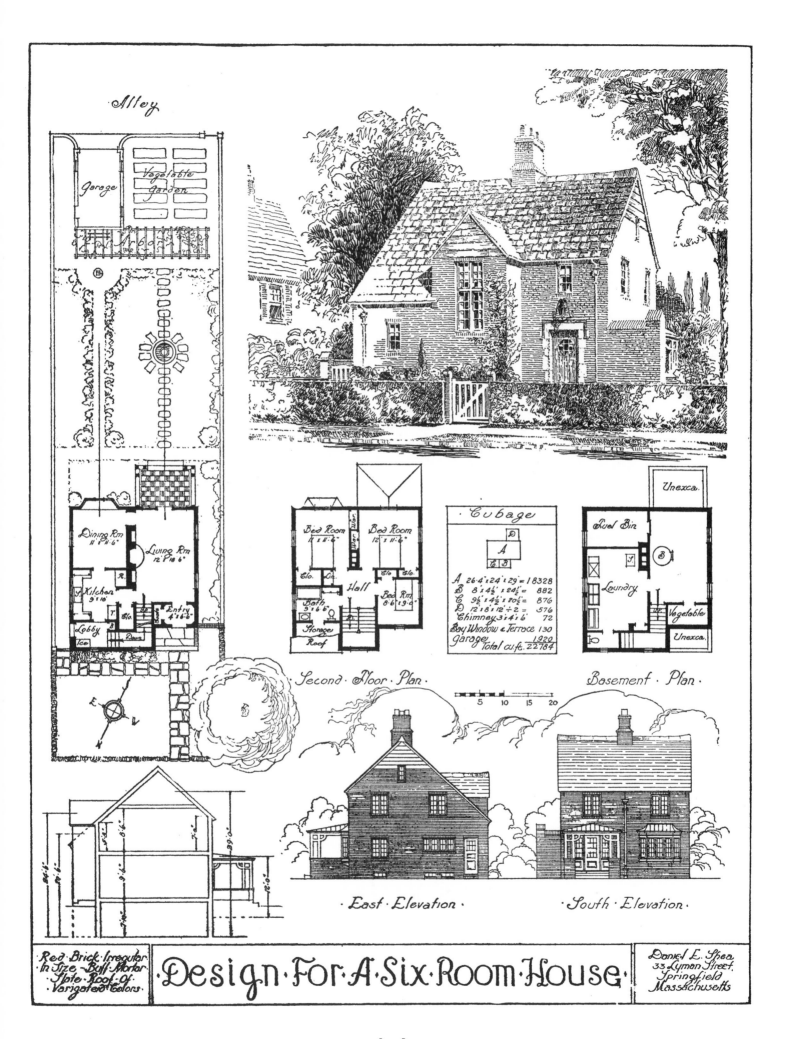

Alley

Garage

Vegetable Garden

Dining Rm
11'×11'6"

Living Rm
12'×18'6"

Kitchen
9'×16'

Lobby

Entry
4'×6'6"

Bed Room
11'×11'6"

Bed Room
12'×11'6"

Hall

Bed Rm
8'6"×9'

Bath
9'6"×6'

Storage
Roof

Second Floor Plan

·Cubage·

A 26'4"×24'×29 = 18328
B 8'×14½'×24½' =   882
C 9½'×14½'×20½' =   876
D 12'×8'×12'÷2 =   576
Chimney 3'×4'×6' =   72
Bay Window & Terrace 130
Garage   1920
Total cu.ft. 22784

Fuel Bin

Unexca.

Laundry

Vegetable

Unexca.

Basement Plan

5 10 15 20

East·Elevation·

·South·Elevation·

Red·Brick·Irregular
In·Size·Buff·Mortar
Slate·Roof·Of·
Variegated·Colors.

·Design·For·A·Six·Room·House·

Daniel L. Shea
33 Lyman Street
Springfield
Massachusetts

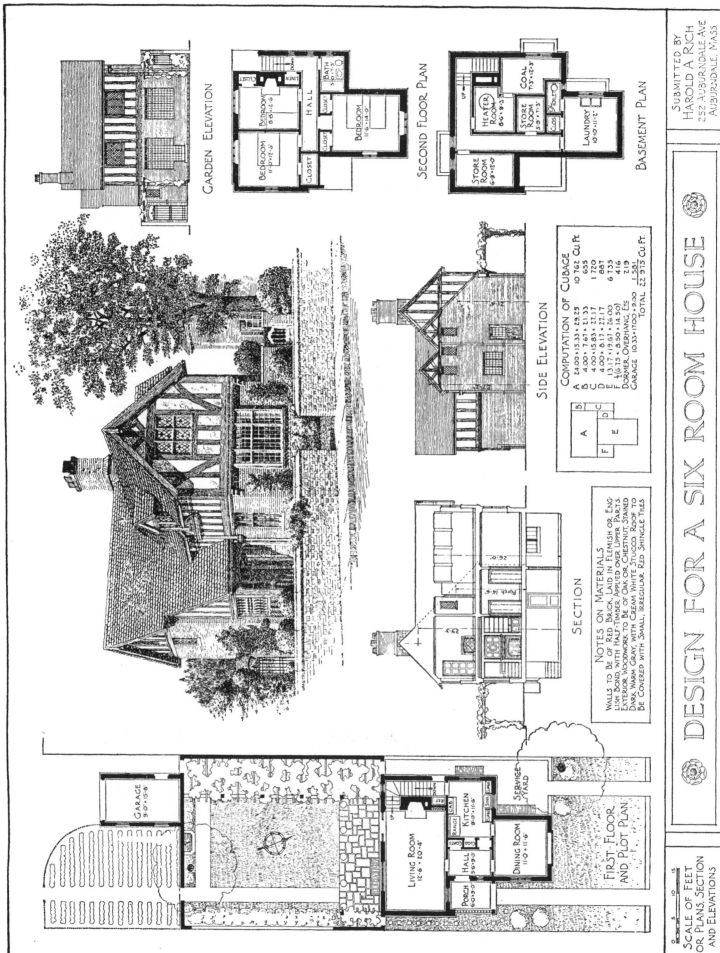

DESIGN FOR A SIX ROOM HOUSE

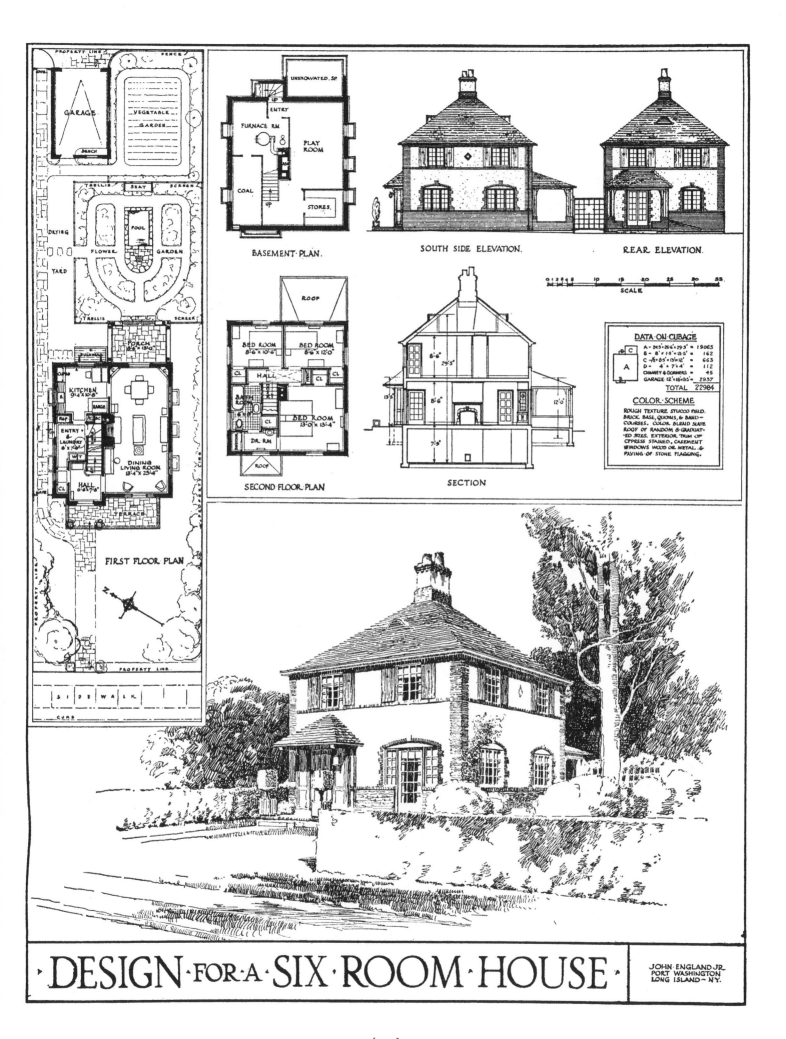

BASEMENT · PLAN.

SOUTH SIDE ELEVATION.

REAR ELEVATION.

SCALE

SECOND FLOOR PLAN

SECTION

FIRST FLOOR PLAN

DATA · ON · CUBAGE

A - 24'3" × 26'6" × 29'3" = 19065
B - 8' × 13 × 13'5" = 162
C - ½ × 8'5" × 13' × 12' = 663
D - 4' × 7' × 4' = 112
CHIMNEY & DORMERS = 45
GARAGE 12' × 18' × 13'5" = 2937
TOTAL 22984

COLOR · SCHEME

ROUGH TEXTURE STUCCO FIELD.
BRICK BASE, QUOINS, & BAND—
COURSES. COLOR BLEND SLATE
ROOF OF RANDOM & GRADUAT—
ED SIZES. EXTERIOR TRIM OF
CYPRESS STAINED. CASEMENT
WINDOWS WOOD OR METAL. &
PAVING OF STONE FLAGGING.

GARAGE

VEGETABLE GARDEN

POOL

FLOWER GARDEN

DRYING YARD

KITCHEN 9'4" × 10'8"

ENTRY & LAUNDRY 6' × 7'0"

HALL 6'6" × 7'6"

DINING LIVING ROOM 13'4" × 25'4"

PORCH 16'6" × 13'0"

TERRACE

FURNACE RM

COAL

PLAY ROOM

STORES.

UNEXCAVATED SP.

ENTRY

ROOF

BED ROOM 8'6" × 10'6"

BED ROOM 8'6" × 12'0"

HALL

BATH ROOM

BED ROOM 13'0" × 13'4"

DR. RM

ROOF

DESIGN · FOR · A · SIX · ROOM · HOUSE

JOHN · ENGLAND JR
PORT WASHINGTON
LONG ISLAND · N·Y.

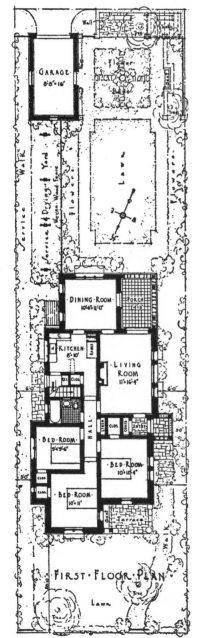

FIRST·FLOOR·PLAN·

- GARAGE 8'8"×16'
- DINING·ROOM 10'6"×11'0"
- PORCH 7'4"×5'
- KITCHEN 8'×10'
- LIVING ROOM 11'×16'4"
- BED·ROOM 9'6"×9'6"
- BED·ROOM 10'6"×12'4"
- BED·ROOM 10'×11'

· EAST · ELEVATION ·

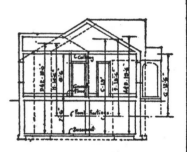

SECTION

GRAPHIC SCALE

· REAR · ELEVATION ·

· CUBAGE ·

Cu.Ft.
A· 22'11'6·15'6" = 7407
B· 23'11'6·15'6" = 7848
C· 12'6"·11'·15'6 = 2654
D· 6'·12'·18'0" = 1296
E· 5'·16'6"·18'0" = 891
F· 7'4"·11'·13'6"½ = 627
G· 4'·5'·12'6"½ = 175
H· 1'·6'·14'6"½ = 87
Total·for·House· 20,985
Garage·16'·18'·5'6" = 1,620 Use·of·Garage
Total = 22,605 Cu.Ft.

NOTES
Walls·to·be·Hollow·Tile·or·Concrete,
Rough·Cement·Finish, with·a·few·Stones
Built·In·Around·the·Base, Blending·Into
the·Stucco ~ Buff·Limestone·or·Sand
Stone·Trim·At·Windows·Slate·Roof
Wood·Trim·Oak·Stained·Dark.
Windows·Metal·Casements·Painted·Green.

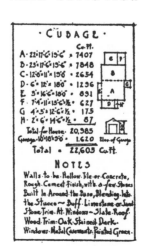

· BASEMENT · PLAN ·

- LAUNDRY
- ENTRY
- FURNACE· ROOM
- PRESERVES
- WORK SPACE
- COAL STORAGE

· DESIGN · FOR · A · SIX · ROOM · HOUSE ·

GEORGE P. AXT
and
CLARENCE B· MACKAY
In·Care·of· G.F. Axt
409·32nd·Street
·Woodcliff·New·Jersey·

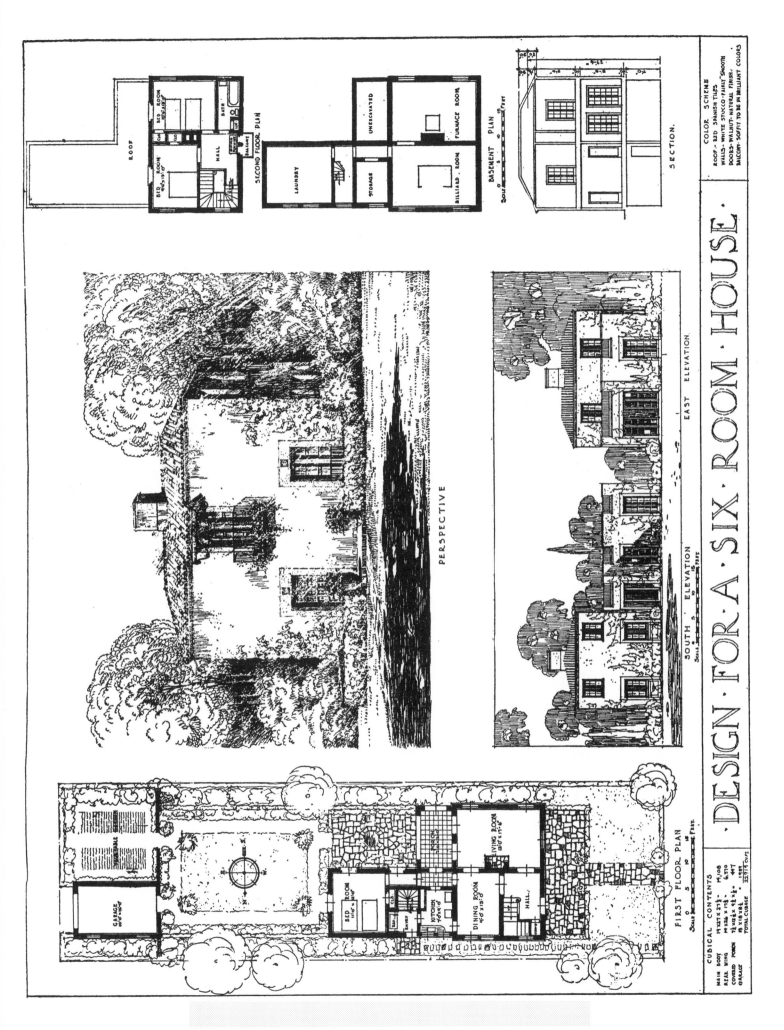

ROOF

BED ROOM

BATH

HALL

SECOND FLOOR PLAN

UNEXCAVATED

FURNACE ROOM

LAUNDRY

STORAGE

BILLIARD ROOM

BASEMENT PLAN

SECTION.

COLOR SCHEME

ROOF - RED SPANISH TILES
WALLS - WHITE STUCCO - FAIRLY SMOOTH
DOORS - WALNUT - NATURAL FINISH -
BALCONY - SOFFIT TO BE IN BRILLIANT COLORS

PERSPECTIVE

EAST ELEVATION

SOUTH ELEVATION

GARAGE

GARAGE

BED ROOM

KITCHEN

PORCH

LIVING ROOM

DINING ROOM

HALL

FIRST FLOOR PLAN

CUBICAL CONTENTS

MAIN BODY
REAR WING
COVERED PORCH
GARAGE
TOTAL CUBAGE

· DESIGN · FOR · A · SIX · ROOM · HOUSE ·

GARAGE
11'×18'6"

TERRACE

LIVING ROOM
14'×20'6"

PORCH
SEAT

BREAKFAST
ROOM

ENTRY

KITCHEN
7'6"×10'

COATS

PORCH

S
E — W
N

BED ROOM
15'×16'

BATH

BED ROOM
10'×14'

CLO SET

CLOSET

LINEN

CLOSET

SECOND FLOOR

A

B

BED ROOM
9'×10'6"

FURNACE ROOM
14'×21'

COAL
5'6"×8'

FRUIT

BASEMENT

LAUNDRY
15'×17'

CUBAGE
A-%×29'×28'4"=13,340
B-18×14'×25'4"=6,360
GAR-8×18×9'=1,3215
TOTAL =21,535
SALMON BRICK
BLUE GREEN &
GREY SLATE
SHINGLES

WEST

0 2 4 6 8 10   20

SOUTH

10'9"

9'6"

8'6"

8'0"

SECTION

12'0"

7'3"

EAST

DESIGN FOR A SIX ROOM HOUSE

JOHN DONALD TUTTLE
2 — WEST — 47TH ST
NEW YORK CITY
THIRTEENTH FLOOR

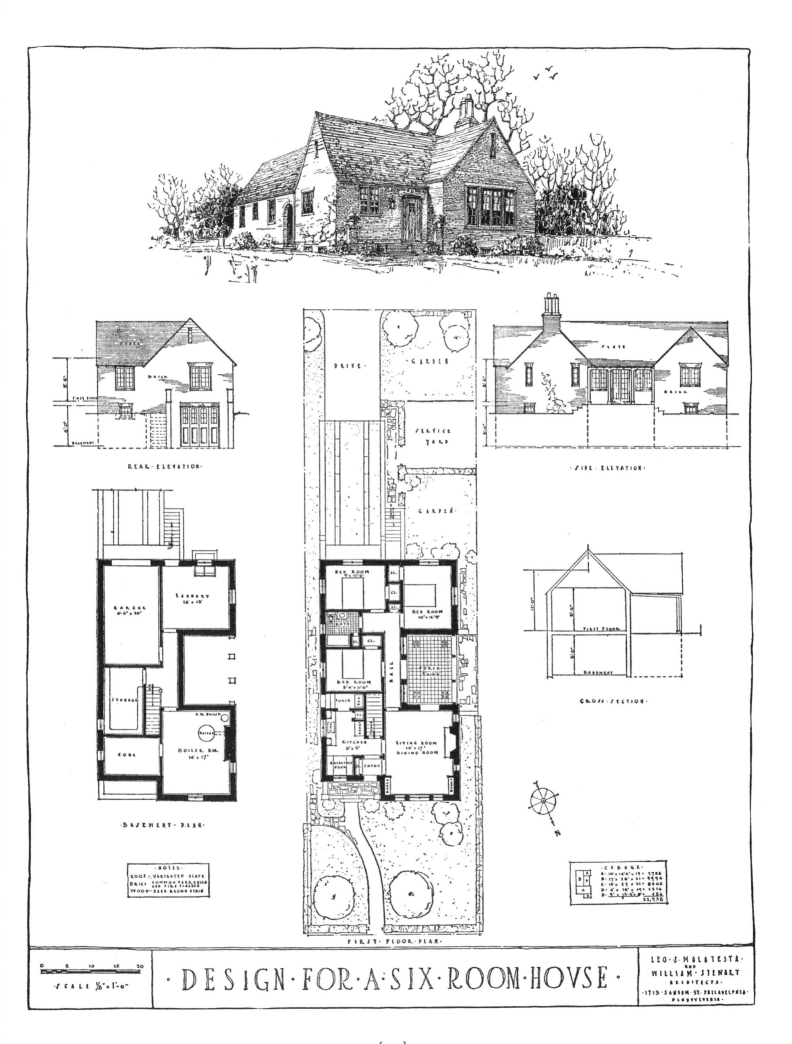

REAR·ELEVATION·

·SIDE·ELEVATION·

CROSS·SECTION·

·BASEMENT·PLAN·

·FIRST·FLOOR·PLAN·

GARAGE 8'·6" x 20'

LAUNDRY 14' x 13'

STORAGE

COAL

H.W. BOILER

BOILER

BOILER RM. 14' x 17'

BED ROOM 9' x 12'·6"

BED ROOM 10' x 12'·9"

BED ROOM 8'·6" x 11'·0"

PORCH

KITCHEN 8' x 9'

BREAKFAST ROOM

ENTRY

LIVING ROOM 14' x 17' DINING ROOM

PORCH

DRIVE

GARDEN

SERVICE YARD

GARDEN

NOTES
ROOF - VARIGATED SLATE
BRICK - COMMON HARD CULLS AND FIRE FLASHES
WOOD - DARK BROWN STAIN

CUBAGE
A · 10' x 14'·6" = 19 · 2788
B · 17' x 28' x 21 · 9996
C · 15' x 27 x 21' · 8505
D · 4' x 14' x 19 · 1216
P · 4' x 13·6' = · 459
22,938

·DESIGN·FOR·A·SIX·ROOM·HOVSE·

SCALE 1/8" = 1'-0"
0 5 10 15 20

LEO·J·MALATESTA·
AND
WILLIAM·STEWART
ARCHITECTS·
·1713·SANSOM·ST·PHILADELPHIA·
PENNSYLVANIA·

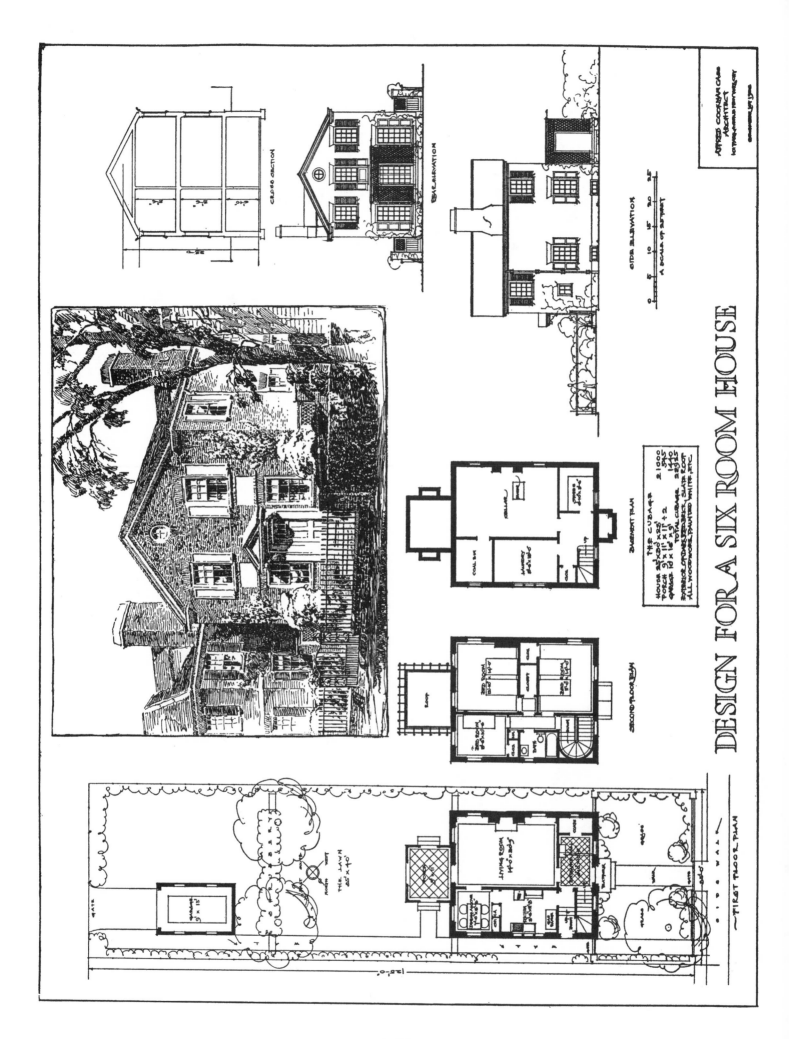

DESIGN FOR A SIX ROOM HOUSE

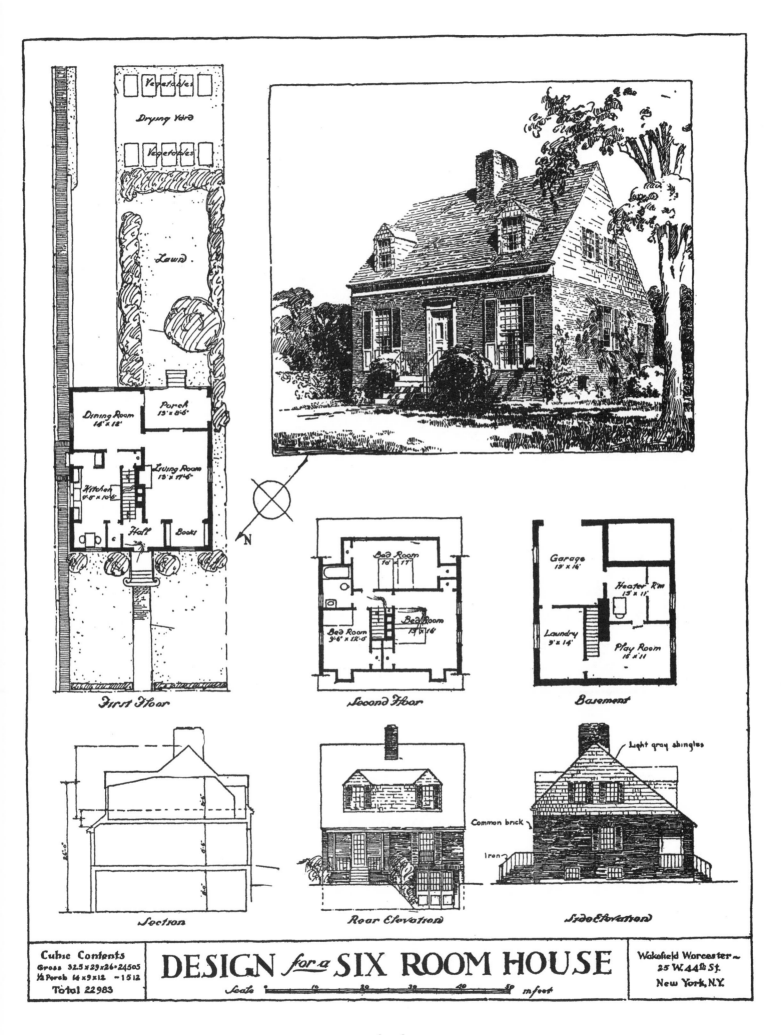

Vegetables

Drying Yard

Vegetables

Lawn

Dining Room
14' x 12'

Porch
13' x 8'-6"

Kitchen
9'-6" x 10'-6"

Living Room
13' x 17'-6"

Hall

Books

N

First Floor

Bed Room
10' x 17'

Bed Room
9'-6" x 12'-6"

Bed Room
14' x 16'

Second Floor

Garage
13' x 16'

Heater Rm
13' x 11'

Laundry
9' x 14'

Play Room
16' x 11'

Basement

Section

Rear Elevation

Light gray shingles

Common brick

Iron

Side Elevation

Cubic Contents
Gross 32.5 x 29 x 26 = 24505
½ Porch 14 x 9 x 12 = 1512
Total 22983

Wakefield Worcester ~
25 W. 44th St.
New York, N.Y.

DESIGN for a SIX ROOM HOUSE

Scale   10   20   30   40   50 in feet

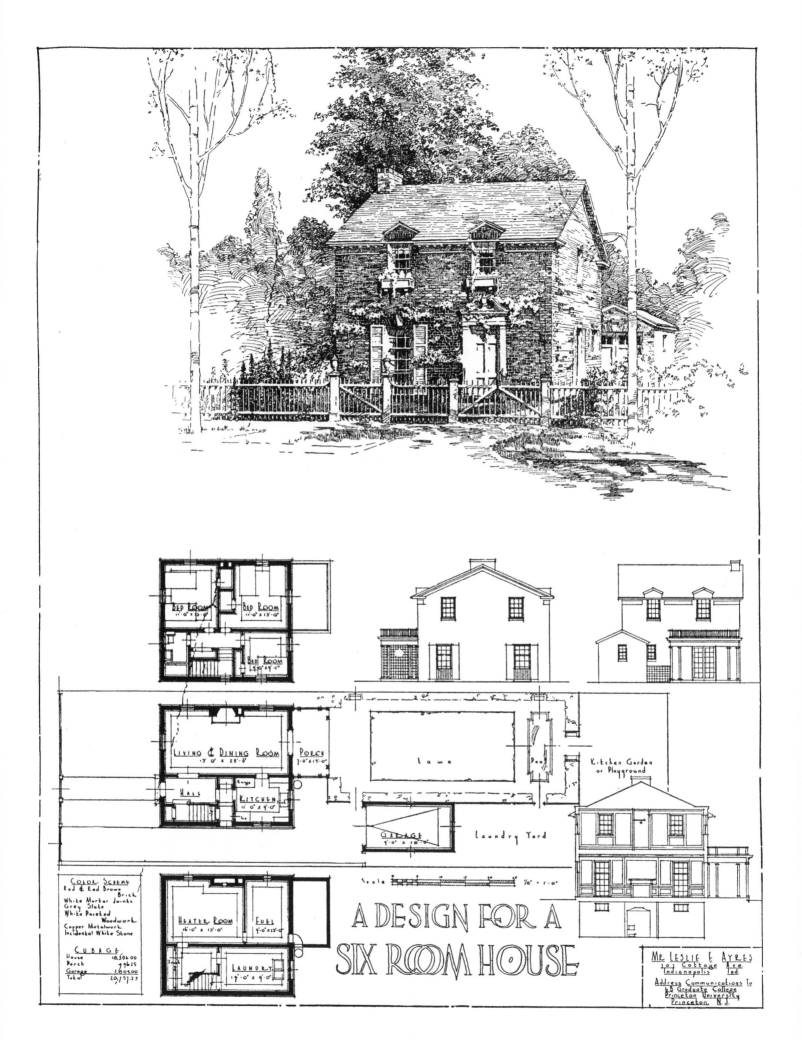

COLOR SCHEME
Red & Red Brown
Brick
White Mortar Joints
Grey Slate
White Painted
Woodwork
Copper Metalwork
Incidental White Stone

CUBAGE
House   18,506.00
Porch   996.25
Garage   1,605.00
Total   20,757.25

BED ROOM
11'-0" x 13'-0"

BED ROOM
11'-0" x 13'-0"

BED ROOM
13'-0" x 19'-0"

LIVING & DINING ROOM
13'-0" x 25'-8"

PORCH
7'-0" x 13'-0"

HALL

KITCHEN
11'-0" x 9'-0"

Range

Lawn

Pool

GARAGE
9'-0" x 18'-0"

Laundry Yard

Kitchen Garden
or Playground

HEATER ROOM
16'-0" x 13'-0"

FUEL
9'-0" x 13'-0"

LAUNDRY
11'-0" x 9'-0"

Scale

A DESIGN FOR A
SIX ROOM HOUSE

MR. LESLIE E. AYRES
207 Cottage Ave.
Indianapolis   Ind.
Address Communications To
b.b Graduate Colleges
Princeton University
Princeton N.J.

Design for A Six Room House

ANTONIO DI NARDO
AND ALVIN HANKE
420 UNION BUILDING
CLEVELAND OHIO.

Basement Plan

Second Story Plan

South Elevation

East Elevation

Section

Scale of Plans

First Story & Plot Plan

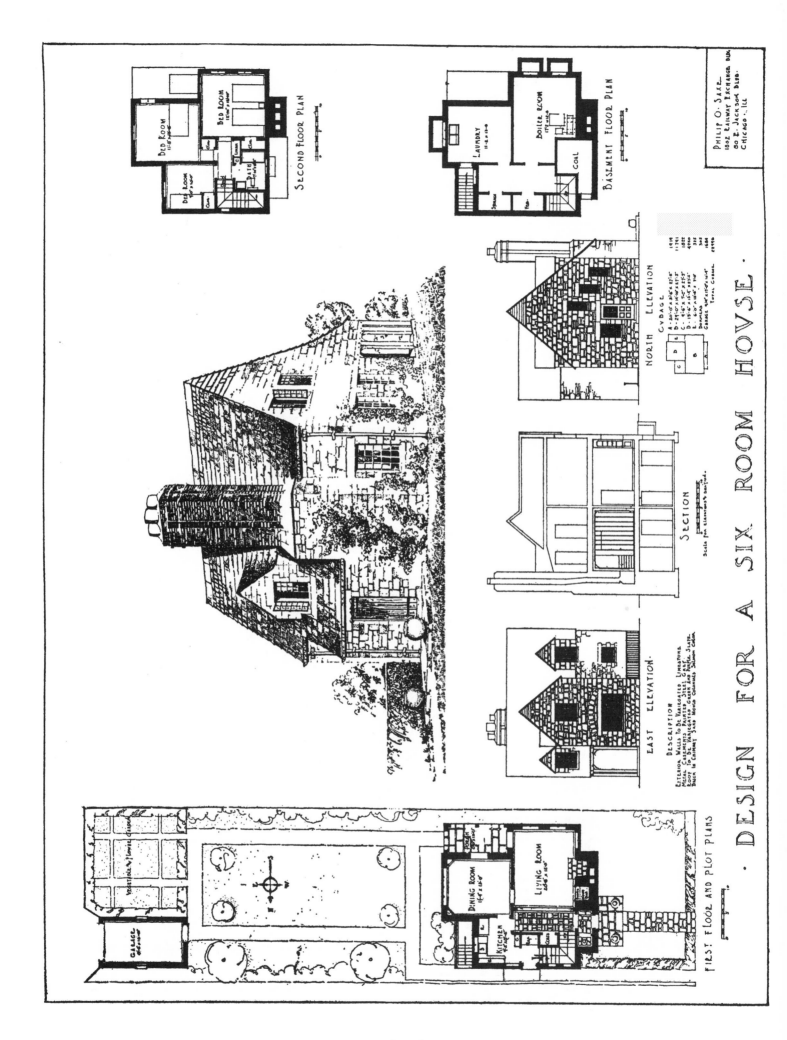

SECOND FLOOR PLAN

BED ROOM

BED ROOM

BED ROOM

BATH

CLOS

CLOS

LINEN

BASEMENT FLOOR PLAN

LAUNDRY

BOILER ROOM

COAL

PHILIP O. SAXE.
1002 RAILWAY EXCHANGE BLDG.
80 E. JACKSON BLVD.
CHICAGO. ILL.

NORTH ELEVATION

CUBAGE

SECTION

EAST ELEVATION

DESCRIPTION

FIRST FLOOR AND PLOT PLANS

GARAGE

VEGETABLE

DINING ROOM

LIVING ROOM

KITCHEN

· DESIGN FOR A SIX ROOM HOUSE ·

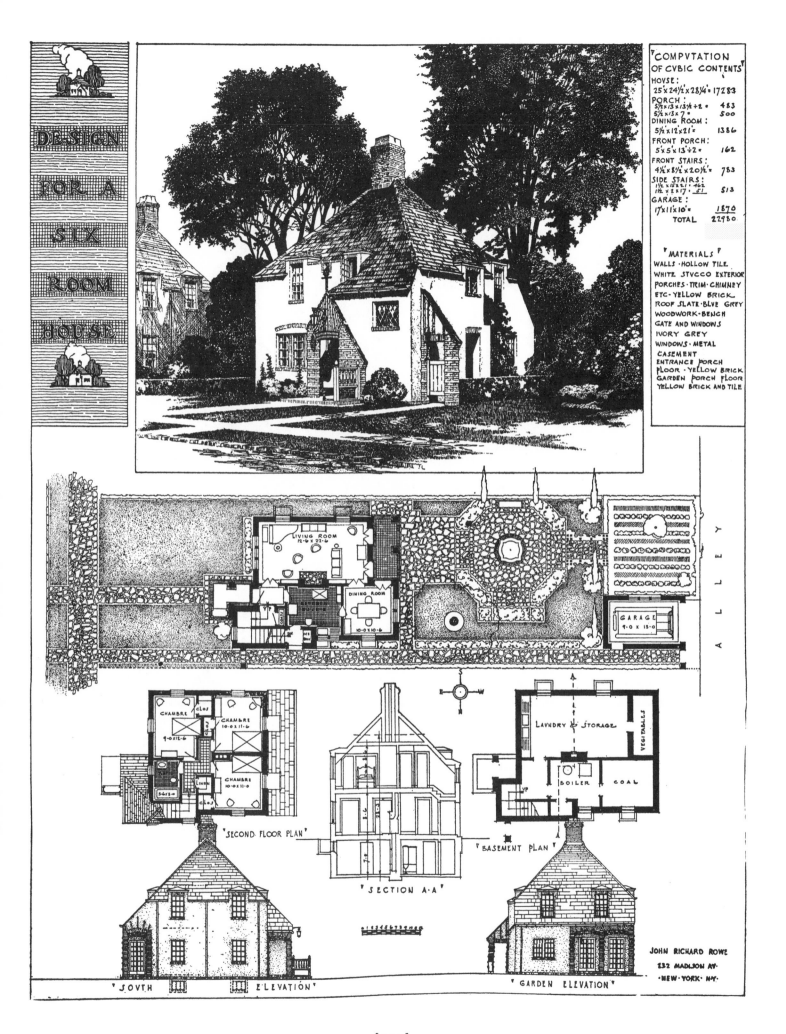

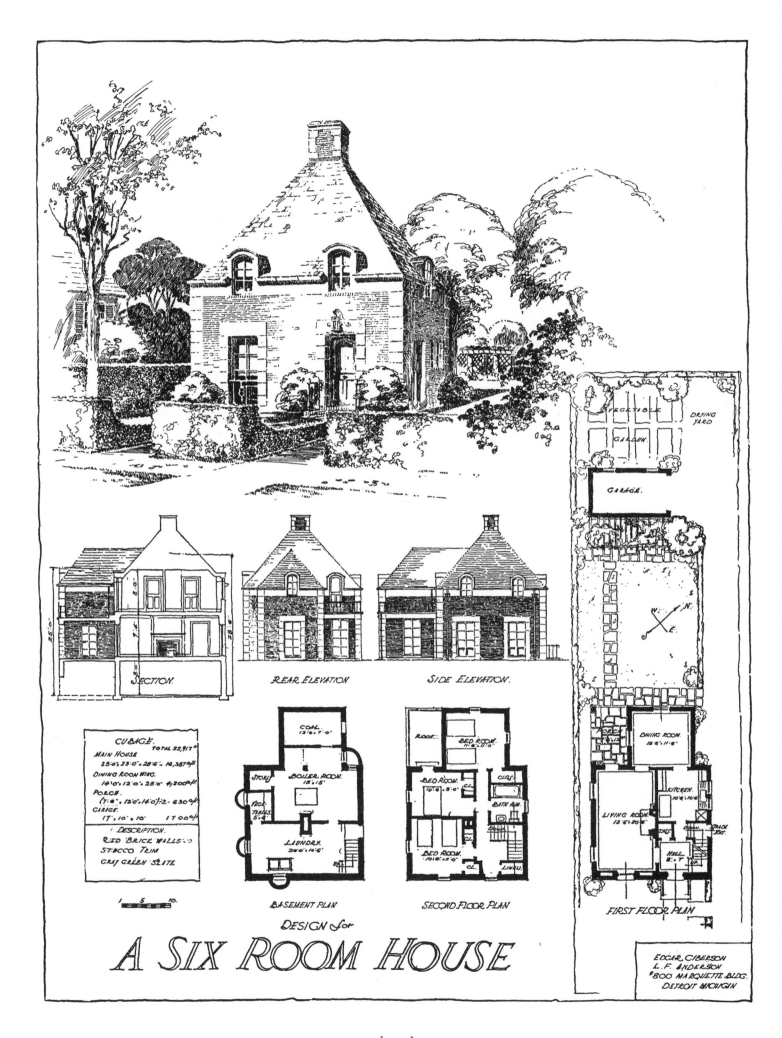

CUBAGE.
TOTAL 22,917°
MAIN HOUSE
25'-0": 23'-0": 28'-6"= 16,387 °ft.
DINING ROOM WING.
14'-0": 12'-0": 25'-0"= 4,200 °ft.
PORCH.
(7'-0": 12'-0": 14'-0"):2= 630 °ft.
GARAGE.
17':10':10'   1700 °ft.

DESCRIPTION.
RED BRICK WALLS
STUCCO TRIM
GRAY GREEN SLATE

SECTION.

REAR ELEVATION

SIDE ELEVATION.

BASEMENT PLAN

SECOND FLOOR PLAN

FIRST FLOOR PLAN

DESIGN for

A SIX ROOM HOUSE

EDGAR CIBERSON
L. F. ANDERSON
800 MARQUETTE BLDG.
DETROIT MICHIGAN

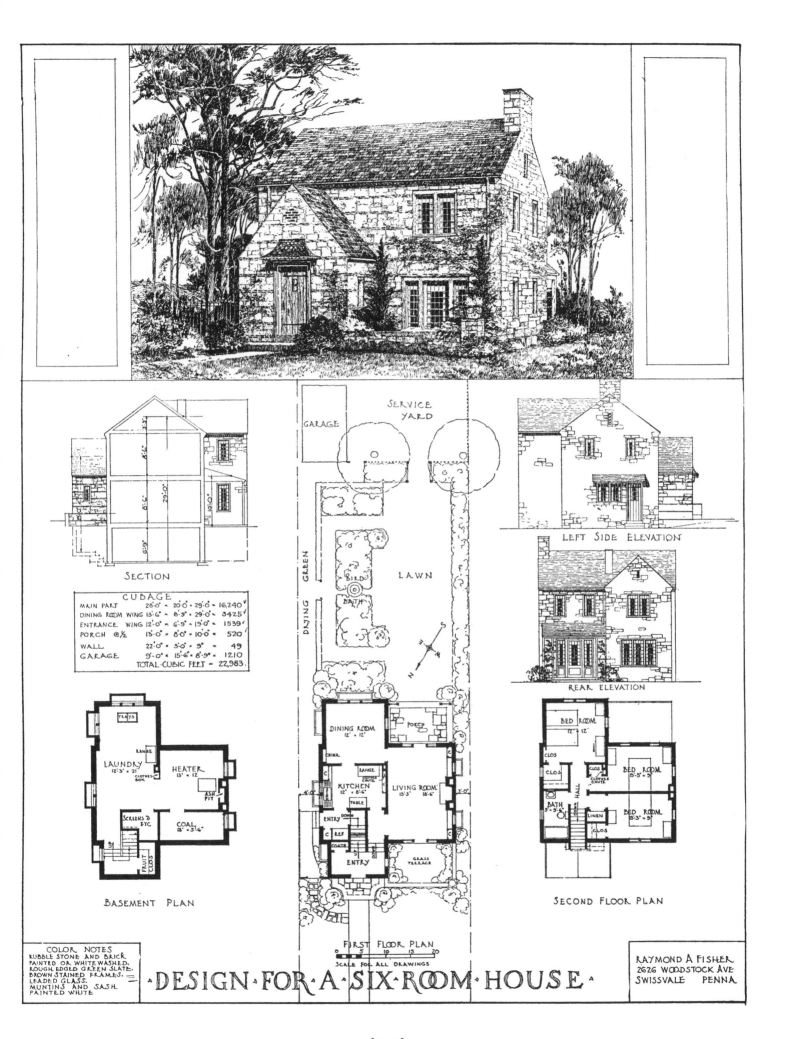

SECTION

CUBAGE

MAIN PART	28'-0" × 20'-0" × 29'-0" =	16,240'
DINING ROOM WING	13'-6" × 8'-9" × 29'-0" =	3425'
ENTRANCE WING	12'-0" × 6'-9" × 19'-0" =	1539'
PORCH @ ½	13'-0" × 8'-0" × 10'-0" =	520'
WALL	22'-0" × 3'-0" × 9" =	49
GARAGE	9'-0" × 15'-6" × 8'-9" =	1210
	TOTAL CUBIC FEET =	22,983

BASEMENT PLAN

LAUNDRY 12'-3" × 21   HEATER 13' × 12

SCREENS & ETC   COAL 13' × 3'-6"

FRUIT CLOS

SERVICE YARD

GARAGE

DINING GREEN

BIRD BATH

LAWN

DINING ROOM 12' × 12'   PORCH

CHINA

RANGE

KITCHEN 12' × 8'-6"   LIVING ROOM 13'-3" × 18'-6"

ENTRY

REF

COATS

ENTRY   GRASS TERRACE

FIRST FLOOR PLAN

SCALE FOR ALL DRAWINGS
0   5   10   15   20

LEFT SIDE ELEVATION

REAR ELEVATION

SECOND FLOOR PLAN

BED ROOM 12' × 12'

CLOS   CLOS   CLOTHES CHUTE

BED ROOM 13'-3" × 9'

HALL

BATH 5'-3"   LINEN

BED ROOM 13'-3" × 9'

CLOS

COLOR NOTES
RUBBLE STONE AND BRICK
PAINTED OR WHITEWASHED.
ROUGH EDGED GREEN SLATE.
BROWN STAINED FRAMES.
LEADED GLASS.
MUNTINS AND SASH
PAINTED WHITE

DESIGN·FOR·A·SIX·ROOM·HOUSE·

RAYMOND A FISHER
2626 WOODSTOCK AVE
SWISSVALE   PENNA

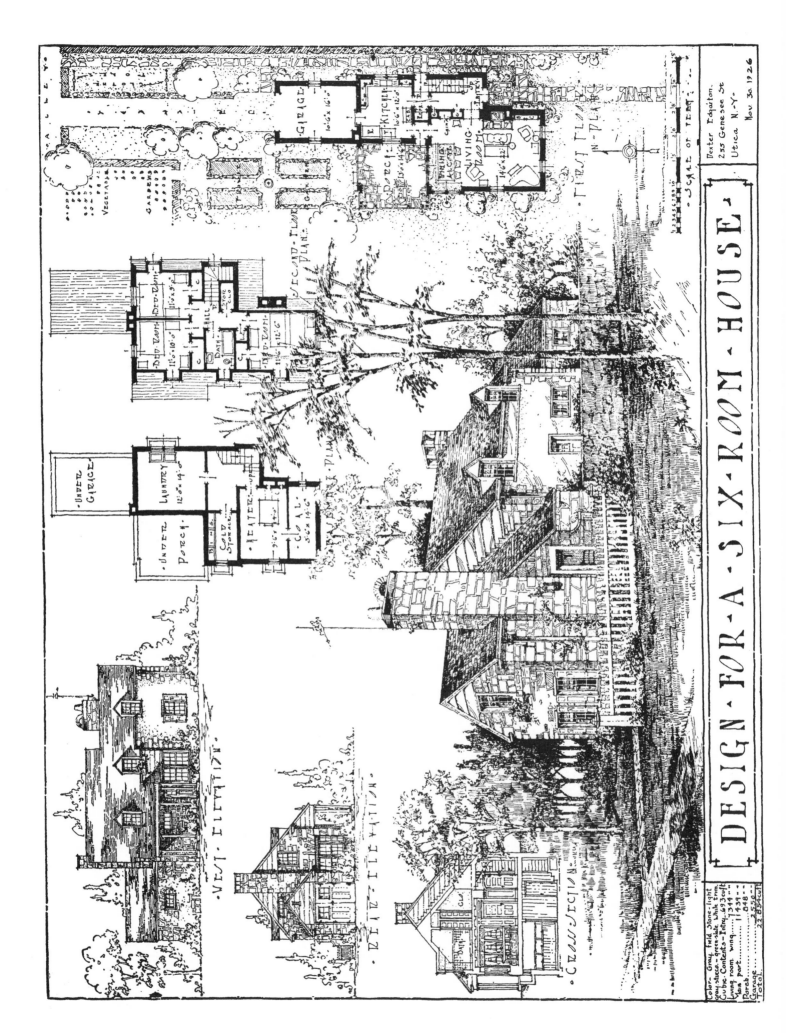

DESIGN·FOR·A·SIX·ROOM·HOUSE·

Dexter Edgerton.
255 Genesee St.
Utica N.Y.
Nov 30 1926

GARDEN

LAWN

PORCH

DINING ROOM
13'-0" x 11'-0"

KITCHEN
11'-0" x 7'-6"

LIVING ROOM
13'-6" x 20'-6"

HALL
11'-0" x 10'-6"

· PLOT PLAN ·

· NORTH ELEVATION ·

REAR ELEVATION

DESIGN FOR A SIX ROOM HOUSE

· SCALE ·

BED ROOM
11'-0" x 11'-0"

BATH

OWNER'S ROOM
13'-3" x 20'-6"

BED ROOM
13'-6" x 10'-3"

SECOND FLOOR PLAN ·

CUBAGE

A = 265 x 25 x 29 = 17340
B = 125 x 7 x 27 = 2362
C = 17 x 7 x 7 = 686
D = 17 x 5.5 x 26 = 2431
TOTAL   22719
        23054

NOTES

WALLS OF COMMON
CHICAGO BRICK ·
GRAY VERGE BOARDS
VARIEGATED SHINGLES

GARAGE
11'-0" x 18'-0"

HALL

UNEXCAVATED
UNDER PORCH

FUEL ROOM
12'-6" x 6'-0"

BOILER R'M
12'-6" x 14'-6"

CELLAR

· BASEMENT PLAN

RALPH W. HAMMETT
245 SEDGWICK ST ·
CHICAGO, · · · ILL

PLAY GROUND

OUR ALLEY

REPAIR
SPACE

GARAGE
9'-0" X 18'

VEGETABLE
GARDEN

OPEN · LAWN ·

KITCHEN
7'-0" X 13'-0"

DOWN UP

HALL
7'-0" X 11'-0"

VEST
5' X 5'

CLOSETS

DINING ROOM
11'-0" X 12'-0"

LIVING ROOM
14'-0" X 20'-0"

SIDE WALK

· SIDE · ELEVATION ·

25'-6" AVERAGE

8'-6"

9'-0"

7'-6"

· SECTION ·

CVBAGE

MAIN HOVSE   19,626
COVERED PORCH   324
GARAGE   2,856
TOTAL C.F.   22,806
~COLORS~
VERIGATED LIGHT RED AND
GOLDEN BROWN BRICK,
BUFF STONE TRIM. ROOF
OF RUSSET BROWN AND
WOOD OF WEATHERED OAK

· REAR · ELEVATION ·

LAUNDRY
10'-6" X 11'-0"

HALL

STORAGE
7'-0" X 12'-6"

FUEL STORAGE
7'-0" X 21'-0"

FURNACE
ROOM
12' X 14'

BASEMENT PLAN

BATH
5' X 8'

BED ROOM
10'-0" X 14'-0"

HALL

BED ROOM
11'-0" X 14'-0"

BED ROOM
10'-0" X 11'-0"

SECOND FLOOR PLAN

Design for a
Six Room Hovse

0   5   10   15
SCALE OF FEET

THAYNE J LOGAN
ARCHITECT·
7610 OLD ORCHARD ROAD
PORTLAND, OREGON

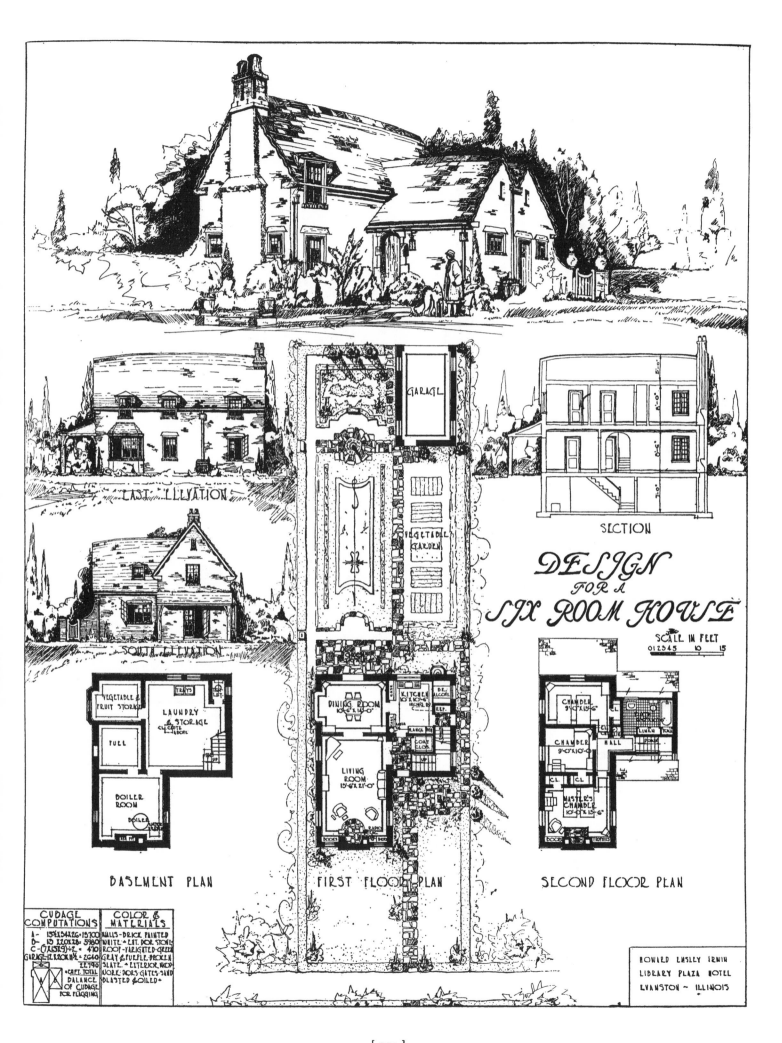

LAST ELEVATION

SOUTH ELEVATION

SECTION

DESIGN
FOR A
SIX ROOM HOUSE

SCALE IN FEET
0 1 2 3 4 5   10   15

GARAGE

VEGETABLE GARDEN

DINING ROOM
10'-6" x 14'-0"

KITCHEN
10'x10'-6"

LIVING ROOM
15'-6" x 21'-0"

CHAMBER
9'-0"x10'-6"

CHAMBER
9'-0"x10'-0"

HALL

MASTER'S CHAMBER
10'-0"x15'-6"

VEGETABLE & FRUIT STORAGE

LAUNDRY & STORAGE

FUEL

BOILER ROOM

BASEMENT PLAN

FIRST FLOOR PLAN

SECOND FLOOR PLAN

HOWARD EMSLEY IRWIN
LIBRARY PLAZA HOTEL
EVANSTON ~ ILLINOIS

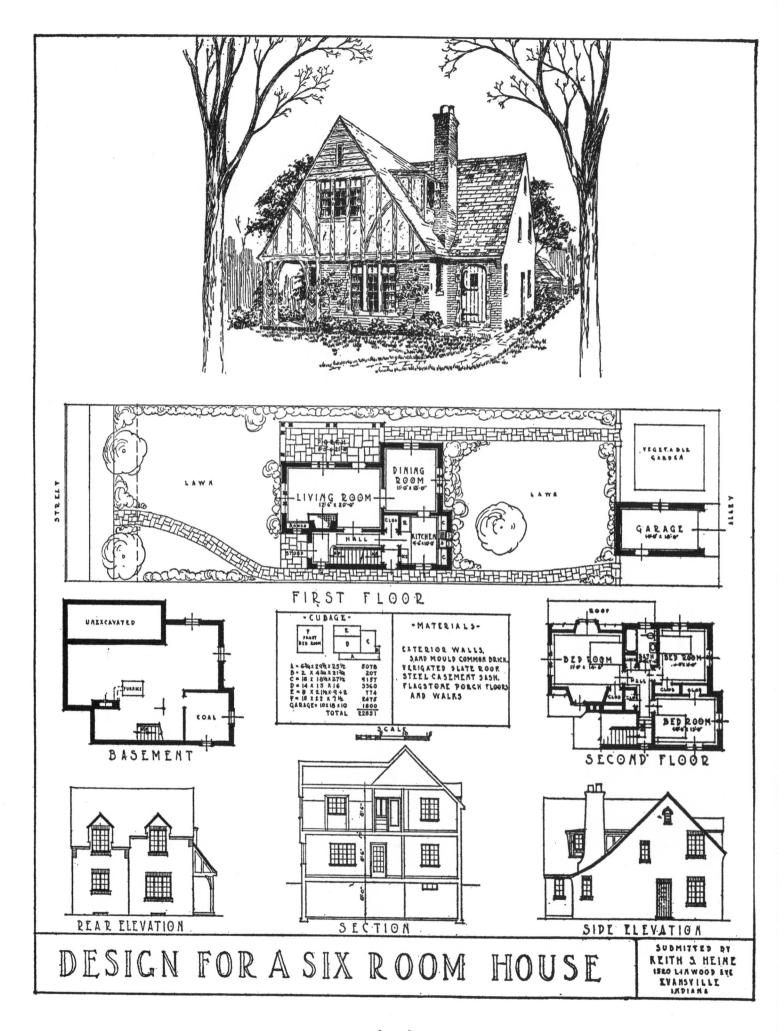

FIRST FLOOR

BASEMENT

SECOND FLOOR

REAR ELEVATION

SECTION

SIDE ELEVATION

DESIGN FOR A SIX ROOM HOUSE

SUBMITTED BY
KEITH J. HEINZ
1520 LINWOOD AVE
EVANSVILLE
INDIANA